The Wind and the Source

The Wind and the Source

In the Shadow of Mont Ventoux

Allen S. Weiss

STATE UNIVERSITY OF NEW YORK PRESS

Published by
State University of New York Press, Albany

Printed in the United States of America

For information, address State University of New York Press, 194 Washington Avenue, Suite 305, Albany, NY 12210-2384

Production by Marilyn P. Semerad
Marketing by Anne M. Valentine

Library of Congress Cataloging-in-Publication Data

Weiss, Allen S., 1953–
The wind and the source : in the shadow of Mont Ventoux / Allen S. Weiss.
p. cm.
Includes bibliographical references and index.
ISBN 0-7914-6489-X (alk. paper)
1. Ventoux Mountain (France)—In literature. 2. Authorship—Psychological aspects. 3. Landscape—History. I. Title.

PN56.3.V47W45 2005
809'.93324492—dc22

2004054168

10 9 8 7 6 5 4 3 2 1

Pour la Chouette

The ancient authors seem to have ignored it.

—Jean-Paul Clébert,
Guide de la Provence Mystérieuse

Contents

Illustrations

All photographs by Allen S. Weiss unless otherwise stated.

Preface

One day the landscape will traverse me.
—Pascal Quignard, *Terrasse à Rome*

What does it mean to love a landscape? Why do certain regions become utopian ideals, such as Provence and Tuscany for so many Americans? Why do certain authors have a predilection for specific landscapes? Why might one be fascinated by a landscape in which one would never wish to live? How does the lay of the land fashion the form of the poem? How does the wind infuse the breath?

Writing of the earliest European translation of *The Arabian Nights,* Richard F. Burton praises it by saying that some compare the tales with "the sudden prospect of magnificent mountains seen after a long desert march: they arouse strange longings and indescribable desires; their marvellous imaginativeness produces an insensible brightening of mind and an increase of fancy-power, making one dream that behind them lies the new and the unseen, the strange and unexpected—in fact, all the glamour of the unknown."[1] *The Wind and the Source: In the Shadow of Mont Ventoux* is a book about a mountain, about the strange and the unknown, about visions and the marvellous. I would hope that it may, like *The Arabian Nights,* stimulate in its readers an insensible brightening of mind and an increase of fancy-power. Yet this book does not speak of the moon rising over the slopes of Mont Ventoux, nor the scent of rosemary and wild thyme; it does not speak of the little Ventoux cheeses flavored with mountain savory that the entomologist Jean-Henri Fabre enjoyed during one of his many ascents of the mountain, nor the extremely rare Tengmalm owl that lives in its woods; it is not about the last wolves seen on the mountain around 1880, nor the charming *mas,* those old farms that encircle the Ventoux, ready for restoration into Provençal dream homes. This is not a book about picturesque, touristic Provence, but about the manifestation of an extreme limit of the imagination that happens to have Provence as its site, as its fantasy-land. This is a book about almost nothing, or rather about a certain nothingness, a veritable void in the symbolic. It is concerned with the vicissitudes of the desire to write *about* a landscape, the desire to write *in* a landscape, and perhaps most curiously, the desire to write *against* a landscape. This is a book about love of the landscape, and abstraction from it.

If, at the outset, the present project had an ideal, it would have been to do for Mont Ventoux what Hokusai accomplished for Mount Fuji in his series of woodblock prints, *Thirty-Six Views of Fuji:* to write a sort of historical novella whose central character is a mountain. But it quickly became apparent that this would be impossible regarding the Ventoux. *The Wind and the Source* in an account of that impossibility, and of how an aesthetic and literary study became a metaphysical quest.

Acknowledgments

I wish to thank Gustaf Sobin for the generous permission to cite excerpts of poems from the following books: *Voyaging Portraits* (New York: New Directions, 1988); *Breaths' Burials* (New York: New Directions, 1995); *Towards the Blanched Alphabets* (Jersey City: Talisman House, 1998).

Cover illustration: Bernard Pagès, *Mont Ventoux* (ink drawing, 2004). This work, created expressly for the cover of *The Wind and the Source,* appears courtesy of the artist.

Paul Cézanne, *Mount Sainte-Victoire,* 1906. Private collection, Zurich, Switzerland. Photo credit: Erich Lessing/Art Resource, NY.

The artist's rendition of the terra-cotta trumpets found on Mont Ventoux is by Susan Willmarth and appears courtesy of the artist.

I

Ascent

> The least shift in syntax, tense-perception,
> would reset the heavens.
>
> —Gustaf Sobin, "A Portrait of the Self as Instrument of Its Syllables"

Roussillon, Friday 17 November 1999, 4:20 P.M. *The only white in the landscape is the peak of Mont Ventoux, the appropriately named Col des Tempêtes [Peak of Storms], rising 1912 meters above the plains of the Vaucluse. Whatever the season, this mountain appears snow covered, hardly what one expects to see in Provence. (The peak is, in fact, covered with snow for about half of each year; for the other half, the limestone scree that blankets the peak above the timberline looks, at a distance, like a snowcap.) Seen from the village of Roussillon, it organizes the picturesqueness of the place by providing an inexorable and singular focal point, and it is rare that it doesn't, in our epoch of infinite photographic representation, solicit at least a casual snapshot. I stroll to the car to get the camera, return, and take one picture, adding to an infinite number of quickly forgotten photographs taken around the globe.*

Roussillon, Friday 17 November 1999, 4:25 P.M. *The white peak disappears, first as approaching clouds mask the sun and throw a vast shadow on the mountain, and then as the upper limits of the Ventoux are almost immediately obscured by a cloud bank, such that mountain and sky merge. It is almost as if the mountain didn't wish to be photographed, resisted representation, wanted to withdraw. Unlike Mount Fuji—everpresent in Japanese culture, even when invisible; of inexhaustible beauty and confounding grace; that absolute object which is the pure and exceedingly complex symbol according to which every other symbol, every other image in Japan, is oriented—Mont Ventoux appears as an empty sign. Empty in its difference from the rest of the landscape: a vast, strange natural monument to something unstated or unknown, its peak a beacon without a message (sign as analogue, unity in a continuum, object in a system, relative difference). Empty due to its sudden and frequent disappearances (sign as digital, unqualified alternation, on/off, one/zero, visible/invisible.) An object needs to disappear in order to become a symbol; yet it is as if the absence of the Ventoux somehow signals its presence—paradoxically, an inexpressible plenitude and an unimaginable emptiness—and nothing more. Mute semaphore, not living metaphor. Mont Ventoux appears as a pure, active principle, a secretive manifestation of* natura naturans.

What follows is an account not, as would be the case in fairytales or myths, about what the mountain says, but about its inscrutable silence.

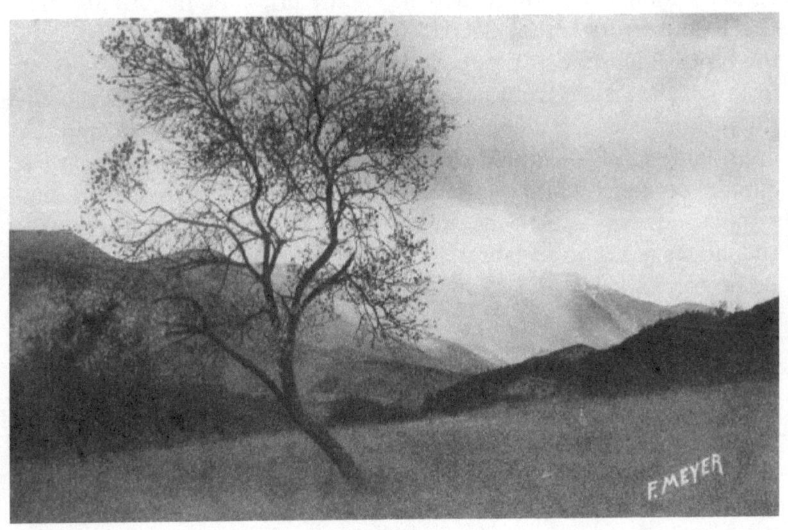

FIGURE 1. Mont Ventoux seen from the Toulourène Valley.

"We came across an elderly shepherd on a slope of the mountain who made every effort with many words to keep us from continuing our climb, saying that fifty years earlier, driven by a like youthful motivation, he had climbed to the very top and had brought back from there nothing but repentance, weariness, and his body and clothing torn by stones and bushes, and that no one had been known before or since to dare undertake a similar climb."[1] So wrote Francesco Petrarch on the evening of 26 April 1336 to his confessor, Dionigio da Borgo San Sepulcro, priest in the Augustinian Order and Professor of Sacred Scripture. Petrarch wrote from the town of Malaucène at the foot of Mont Ventoux—the highest point in Provence, visible from nearly everywhere in the region, seemingly the prototype of the sacred mountain. The words, prophetic and disapprobative, of this unidentified shepherd constitute the earliest extant record of Mont Ventoux: a negative depiction of the mountain, suggesting desolation, emptiness, danger.[2] We neither know the shepherd's name nor celebrate his exploit, but his warning should not be forgotten, since in a strange way it informs the future history of the mountain.

One might well imagine that Mont Ventoux would have offered an ideal site for a hermitage devoted to ascetic meditation, even mortification. But Petrarch would make of it something quite different. Having disregarded the shepherd's warnings, Petrarch—his "delicate mind, seeking honorable delight"—along with his brother and their servants, made the ascent of the "Windy Mountain." Visible from every direction, Mont Ventoux had long offered Petrarch—who had lived in the region since childhood—a challenge, and one that was recently resuscitated by his reading in Titus Livy's *History of Rome* of how King Philip of Macedonia ascended Mount Hemo in Thessaly. From the summit of Mount Hemo it was believed that one could see both the Adriatic Sea and the Black Sea, a vista worthy of a conqueror's ambitions. Petrarch's conquest would be otherwise, and would give him the honor of being the first post-classical writer with a marked taste for landscape views. Petrarch expresses the ascent in allegorical terms already ancient. For those who seek the heights, the road is long and the burden heavy. Furthermore, while some (like his brother) ardously attain the peaks by traversing perilous ridges, others (like Petrarch) attempt easier paths, lazily meandering through

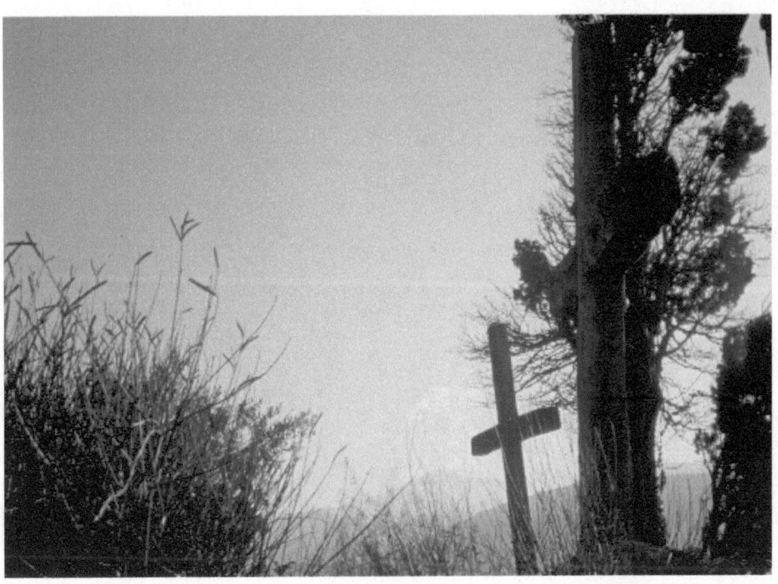

FIGURE 2. Mont Ventoux seen from Malaucène.

valleys, descending as often as ascending, creating a veritable labyrinth of the slopes. Yet how, indeed, can one reach a summit by descending!? Realizing his error, Petrarch finally attains the peak, reproaching himself in allegorical terms:

> What you have experienced so often today in trying to climb this mountain you should know happens to you and to many others as they approach the blessed life. This is not easily realized by men, however, because although the movements of the body are visible, the movements of the mind are invisible and concealed. The life we call blessed is certainly located on high, and, as it is said, a very narrow road leads to it. Many hills also intervene and one must proceed from virtue to virtue with very deliberate steps. At the summit lies the end of all things and the limit of the path to which our traveling is directed.[3]

With altitude comes that rarefaction which shortens the breath, lightens the mind, and inspires the soul, whence the feeling of an "eternal instant" in the heart of the present, experienced by so many mountain

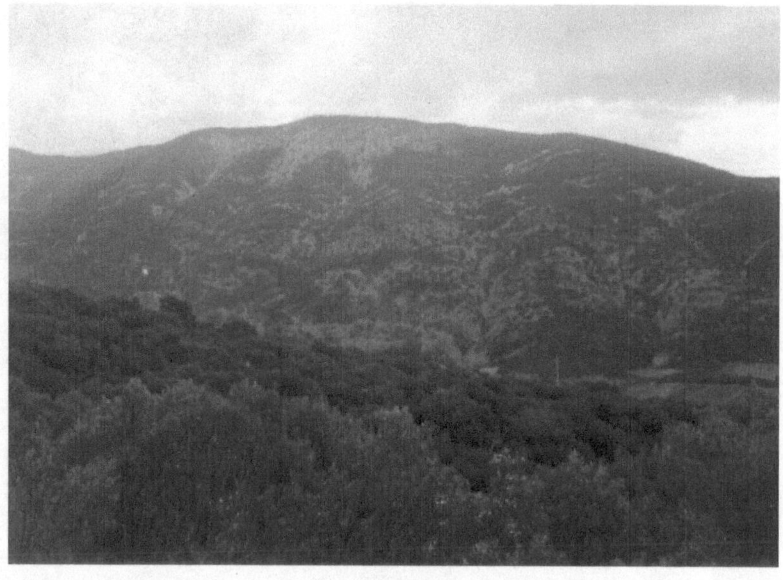

FIGURE 3. Mont Ventoux, slopes.

climbers. Either reach the summit or risk the abyss. But the summit must be attained with mind, not body; ephemeral, earthly pleasures must give way to immortal, spiritual truths. For every geography bears a point at which reality departs, and every site offers metaphors for both immanence and transcendence. The verticality of the monolith has always been a mark of the sacred: from the tumuli and cairns of the pagans through the holy mountains of the great polytheistic religions, culminating in those peaks sacred to the monotheistic faiths, the mountain is the *axis mundi,* connecting heaven, earth, and underworld. Uncover the layers of metaphor incrusted upon a landscape, and one will find a god.

At the summit, fascintated by the unrestricted spectacle, Petrarch stands as in a trance: "Clouds were beneath me. And suddenly what I had heard and read about Athos and Olympus became less incredible to me when I looked out from this mountain of lesser fame."[4] Allegorically situating the Ventoux between one of the holiest peaks of Christiandom and the sacred mount of the Greek gods, Petrarch senses a nearly indescribable joy. As the sun was already slowly beginning to set, and the moment of descent neared, Petrarch looked

FIGURE 4. View from peak of Mont Ventoux.

around at what he had come to see: "The boundary between Gaul and Spain, the Pyrenees, cannot be seen from there not because anything intervenes as far as I know, but because the human sight is too weak. However, the mountains of the province of Lyons could be seen very clearly to the right, and to the left the sea at Marseille and at the distance of several days the one that beats upon Aigues-Mortes. The Rhone itself was beneath my eyes."[5] The description becomes hyperreal, almost hallucinatory, too lucid, too vast: the mountaintop is a panopticon, revealing the far reaches of the land, roughly equivalent to the limits of Provence and Languedoc.

Visibility is but a metaphor for vision, and Petrarch is seeking loftier things. Suddenly remembering that he had with him a copy of Saint Augustine's *Confessions* (given to him by his confessor), he opens it at random and reads: "And they go to admire the summits of mountains and the vast billows of the sea and the broadest rivers and the expanses of the ocean and the revolutions of the stars and they overlook themselves."[6] As is so often the case, the mountain manifests its *genius loci,* the spirit of the place, through a revelation: the topos of this revelation is precisely the point where mountain and

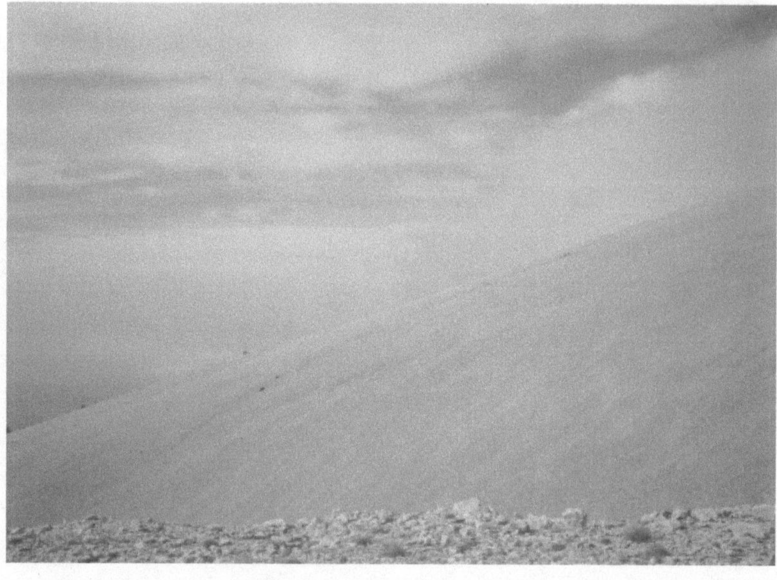

FIGURE 5. Mont Ventoux, scree.

sky meet, a point of mystical fusion of the elements. Attaining the peak motivates the climber to abandon his physical situation and reorient himself towards a transcendental state. The world need disappear for the inner vision to reveal itself. In this Dantesque spectacle, the hyperreal becomes the unreal, evaporating into the truly real, that is, the absolute, the mystical.

Petrarch's inner vision was preconditioned by the Bible, as refracted through Augustine. But for Petrarch, the revelation evinces a double effacement: that of *the mountain itself before the soul* (for what is higher is inner), and that of *the soul before its god* (for what is inner is sacred). It is as if the mountain catapulted Petrarch into transcendence, a transcendence which, in the Christian context, is congruent with immanence, with the innate site of faith. Along with the mountain disappears the vanity of the world. For even the highest mountain is ephemeral, its grandeur sheer *vanitas*. The mountain is not even as dust. Such is a well-tempered transcendence, where sublimation takes the form of dematerialization and iconoclasm, both manifested in opposition to the mountain. A devout Christian, Petrarch cannot sacralize Mont Ventoux, as people of other faiths had done before him; nor can he make a sacrifice on the mountain, for the biblical era of sacrifice is past. So instead, *he sacrifices the mountain itself,* a secret sacrifice to his god, to his poetry, to his soul. The mountain was abolished for the sake of the imagination.

As if in surreal continuation of the hyperreal state of fascination at the summit, the mountain now appears to Petrarch as if but a cubit high, and he makes the descent with his mind's eye turned inward, immersed in harmonious and sacred inspiration. This vision is striking: it is as if the landscape were reduced to one of those medieval Byzantine or Italian images, where the mountain—an artifice of grotesque, broken, stepped terraces—is so small that the depicted saint is of the same height, and easily peers over the peak. In Petrarch's account, the Ventoux is first glorious then insignificant, wondrous then denigrated, breathtaking then deformed. Yet this transformation bears a certain amount of equivocation; it is more than just a rhetorical expression of Petrarch's revelation or a conventional means of depreciating the world, since it partakes of a profound shift in the experience of nature that originated during Petrarch's lifetime. Even if the fourteenth-century experience of the sublime is still primarily relegated to the deity, a new wonder is manifested at the natural world; even if the aesthetic is still limited to the beautiful, a new fascination arises before the grotesque; even if poetry is still centered on the spiritual, novel psychological nuances and increasing attention to detailed description arise. If Petrarch felt the need to shrink the Ventoux—first beautifully described in realist rigor, then imagined as a grotesque miniature—to the size of stage decor, it was in order to reconcile what he would have felt as contradictory needs: love of nature and love of God. The Ventoux exists for him in its full duplicity: natural wonder and artificial simulacrum of the imagination. It has been widely noted that Petrarch's letter on the ascent of Mont Ventoux contains the first post-classic appreciation of a landscape view in and for itself, however much the description is couched in the theological tradition. Neglected, however, is the fact that his representation of the Ventoux is twofold and equivocal: first a realist description of the landscape, then an integral part of an allegory of religious revelation.[7] It is as if the two representations of the Ventoux, realist and allegorical, coalesced into that sort of irrational or paradoxical perspective typical of the epochs before the early Renaissance reinvention of one-point linear perspective, that is to say a perspective that combines multiple points of view and incompatible

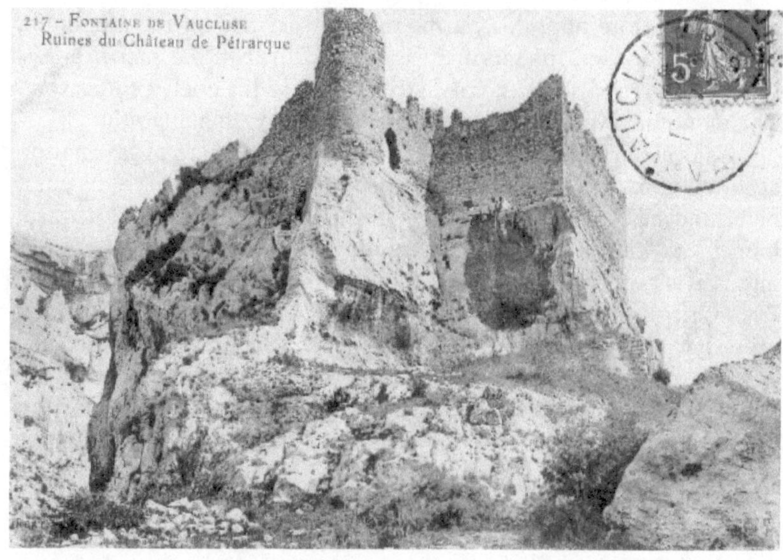

FIGURE 6. Ruins of the chateau of the Bishops of Cavaillon (improperly referred to as the chateau of Petrarch).

pictorial features: conflicting scales, inconsistent lighting, incompatible objects, contradictory styles. This representational amalgamation is fully expressive of the existential paradoxes that defined the era, where a single image may simultaneously serve classical, biblical, descriptive, and decorative purposes. The effects of this hermeneutic complexity on art and poetry are well expressed by Derek Pearsall and Elizabeth Salter in *Landscapes and Seasons of the Medieval World:* "If we can say that in Virgil the reality of landscape is an integral aspect of the interpretation of reality as a whole, for the Middle Ages we must say that natural phenomena are available, in more or less stereotyped form, as a mode of expression for an interpretation of reality which transcends or even denies those phenomena[. . . .] The fluctuations between allegorical, symbolic and typological landscape depend on the immediate pressures of that interpretation. They depend also on the nature of the poem."[8] For Petrarch, landscape description exists in the context of both the expression of worldly reality and the transcendentally based denial of that very same reality. Theologically, the disappearance of the Ventoux would imply a

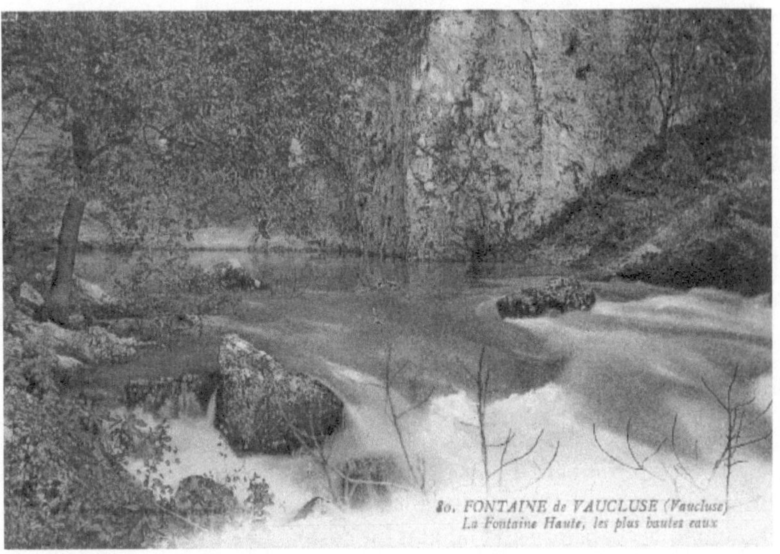

FIGURE 7. Fontaine-de-Vaucluse.

valorization of transcendence; practically, it would permit the displacement of Petrarch's sensitivity to nature onto another milieu, one more propitious to his quotidian and writerly needs. For Petrarch was not to become a saint upon a mountain. But how does this effect the destiny of Mont Ventoux?

The philosopher Maurice Merleau-Ponty, attempting to fathom the profound relations between the flesh of the body, language, and the world, sees symbolic overdetermination such that all objects, great or small, may obtain metaphysical import: "any entity can be *accentuated* as an emblem of Being."[9] Mont Ventoux would seem to be an exception to this rule as it is continually obfuscated, as it perpetually withdraws. At the point where Petrarch concludes his letter describing the ascent, it would appear that the allegory is complete, and the hermeneutic circle closed: from Dionigio da Borgo San Sepulcro's gift to Augustine's wisdom, from Philip of Macedonia's worldly ambitions and the anonymous shepherd's cynicism to Petrarch's revelation, from profane to sacred, from immanence to transcendence, from self to God. But for Petrarch, the mountain could not become metaphor, since the highest things cannot be effectually metaphorized. The Ventoux resists metaphorization. Its emptiness is not that of a floating signifier, magical, open, ready to take on any signification. To the contrary, it is so massive, opaque, anchored, that it absorbs all signification, like a black hole. It is a mountain that does not participate in the Zen parable: before enlightenment, a mountain is just a mountain; during the quest for enlightenment, a mountain is everything but a mountain; after enlightenment, a mountain is once again only a mountain. The Ventoux is the anti-Fuji.[10] The Ventoux is resolutely uncircumscribable; its symbolic barrenness, desolateness, desertedness is absolute.

For much of his creative life Petrarch lived beneath the cliffs of Fontaine-de-Vaucluse, a point from which the Ventoux is invisible. However, mountains would come to constitute one of the central tropes in Petrarch's work; not only his poetry, which abounds in mountain metaphors, but also his essays and letters. Petrarch wrote *De vita solitaria* [The Life of Solitude, 1346] to try and convince his friend Philippe de Cabassolle, Bishop of Cavaillon, to move back to Fontaine-de-Vaucluse and inhabit his castle, which dominated the village. As an argument, Petrarch proffers the praise, in the words of Seneca, of both the sources of great rivers and that feeling of almost religious mystery caused by deep caves upon mountain cliffs, thus linking mountains to both religious sentiment and poetic inspiration.[11] This latter symbol conflates Petrarch's two major topoi, the mountain and the grotto. In *Secretum* [My Secret, 1347]—an allegorical autobiography in the form of an imaginary discussion with Saint Augustine, his spiritual guide to Mont Ventoux—Petrarch situates Truth on a mountaintop. The metaphors are the same: one must leave the beaten path, the plains can be freely seen only from the top of the hill, the earthly body must be abandoned, and the soul must ascend to the heavens. Yet he writes not of Mont Ventoux, but the Atlas Mountains, the site of his vast epic poem, *Africa*. In the words of Horace, Petrarch offers an image comparable to the central icon of both the Gothic and romantic sensibilities:

> The tallest trees most fear the tempest's might,
> The highest towers come down with most affright,
> The loftiest hills feel first the thunder smite.[12]

For Petrarch, as for so many following the Christian tradition, the mountain would be a privileged topos of inspiration; however, as he already knew from his famous ascent, it is not without risk and anguish that the summit is conquered. Petrarch's relation to the Church was in great part determined by his identification with Augustine. This is clearly stated in *Secretum,* where the narrator, Francesco, speaking of his interlocutor, the Augustine of the *Confessions,* admits: "I seem to be hearing the story of my own self, the story not of another's wandering, but of my own."[13] Yet however powerful this identification, Petrarch's path decidedly diverged from that of Augustine, and Petrarch's metaphors were put to very different uses. For all identification is misidentification, whence the origins of literary creativity.

In his letter on the ascent of Mont Ventoux, the citation from Augustine's *Confessions,* "And they go to admire the summits of mountains . . . ," was transformed, above all else, into an allegory to express the state of Petrarch's soul. The "sacrifice" of Mont Ventoux was a precondition of his self-revelation. But what did these very same lines mean to Augustine? The saint continues in this state of wonder that men, in their fascination with the world around them, might overlook themselves: "They do not marvel at the thought that while I have been mentioning all these things, I have not been looking at them with my eyes, and that I could not even speak of mountains or waves, rivers or stars, which are things that I have seen, or of the ocean, which I know only on the evidence of others, unless I could see them in my mind's eye, in my memory, and with the same vast spaces between them that would be there if I were looking at them in the world outside myself."[14] What Petrarch elides is the fact that this citation appears, in the tenth book of the *Confessions,* within the context of Augustine's analysis of memory. The mountain in question is unreal, a mere appearance; it exists not without but within, as a sensory image imprinted on the mind, as memory. The true panopticon is not a site in the world, nor the sight of the world, but the power of the imagination. And yet, however abstract this particular passage on sensory experience and its resultant memory may appear within the context, for Augustine it is imbued with both a profound attachment to spiritual transcendence and a passionate, pathetic dramatization of earthly love. One need only turn back to the eighth book of the *Confessions,* the culminating scene of his fierce inner struggle between earthly temptation and spiritual truth. In the summer of the year 386, as he begins to lose control of himself, as his speech disintegrates and his gestures become uncontrollable, as the very existence of the world becomes uncertain, he takes refuge in the small garden of his house in

Milan. This is the scene of his grief, his madness, his transfomation, his salvation: "I was dying a death that would bring me to life."[15] Frantic, violent, agonizing, he knew that to complete the journey all that was required was an act of volition. Whence such will? "Why does this strange phenomenon occur?"[16] He was at odds with himself, rent asunder in a "monstrous state," a Manichean split between two wills—carnal and spiritual—a will cleaved between the residual evil of primordial sin induced in the world's first garden, and that goodness which is the sacred meaning of existence. To do or not to do? At the height of anguish and despair, in a torrent of tears, he went out into the garden and sat under a fig tree. This would be the site of his revelation and salvation, for he heard the voice of a little child from a nearby house repeat, over and over, as if speaking to him alone, "tolle, lege; tolle, lege" (Take up and read). Remembering that Saint Anthony had been admonished by a public reading of the gospel, Augustine opened the Bible at random and fell upon the Pauline epistles, reading words as if addressed expressly to himself: "Not in revelling and drunkenness, not in lust and wantonness, not in quarrels and rivalries. Rather, arm yourselves with the Lord Jesus Christ; spend no more thought on nature and nature's appetites."[17] He was saved, and received his baptism at the hands of Saint Ambrose in 387. Augustine entered the City of God through the portal of his garden.

It was another garden—that of the house he shared with his mother in Ostia, awaiting their sea voyage to return to Africa in the year 387—that would be the scene of Augustine's greatest pathos. Referring to that fateful moment, Augustine writes of that supremely mystical exchange with his mother that took place in an all so worldly garden:

> Our conversation led us to the conclusion that no bodily pleasure, however great it might be and whatever earthly light might shed lustre upon it, was worthy of comparison, or even of mention, beside the happiness of the life of the saints. As the flame of love burned stronger in us and raised us higher towards the eternal God, our thoughts ranged over the whole compass of material things in their various degrees, up to the heavens themselves, from which the sun and the moon and the stars shine down upon the earth. Higher still we climbed, thinking and speaking all the while in wonder at all that you have made. At length we came to our own souls and passed beyond them to the place of everlasting plenty, where you feed Israel

> for ever with the food of truth. There life is that Wisdom by which all these things that we know are made, all things that ever have been and all that are yet to be.[18]

This ascent—which necessitated no mountain, which elided all body—resulted in a moment of total spiritual love for his mother and ecstatic mystical union with God, where the soul is silent and the "dreams and the visions of his imagination spoke no more."[19] The soul of Augustine was transfigured, and his mother was converted. Five days later she died. Such is the ascent, the love, the death, all occluded by the abstract considerations of memory in book ten, a philosophical work of mourning. *This* sad and dramatic ascent is the secret behind Petrarch's revelation, the pathos masked by his own very different, very wordly longings.

For Augustine, it is not the garden that constitutes true sanctuary, but memory, that "vast, immeasurable sanctuary," containing earth and heaven, circumscribing the self.[20] When in book ten Augustine relegates the entirety of the material world to memory, he does so from the position of one who has gained the spiritual world. The remembrance of the ascent evokes both the *specific* pathos regarding his mother's death augmented by the ecstasy of his mystical union with God, and the *general* sense of eschewing the vanity of the world, to celebrate true faith. Neither the garden of immanence nor the mountain of transcendence are of any consequence; neither the dividedness of the will nor the perils of the journey are of any actuality. As the ultimate proof of his spiritual rebirth, even the trauma of his mother's all-too-earthly death has been subsumed by a work of mourning that owes its mental space to memory itself, the proper place of all things of this earth. Such is true faith.

Augustine's relation to landscape might be considered in terms of what Chris Fitter, in his study *Poetry, Space, Landscape,* considers the "ascetic sublime," where the horror of abominable, extreme landscapes—imposing, vast, remote, wild—serves religion as both a means of mortification and a mark of worldly vanity. "The stupendous in landscape is sought only for contemptuous eclipse by the pure *virtus* of an indomitable mental transcendence."[21] Nature may be seen either in the light of a perfect creation or as corrupted by the Fall. A certain tradition of biblical exegesis deems mountains to be horrifying flaws upon the earth, deformed excrescences that are warnings against human ambition, pride, and hubris. Their extravagant,

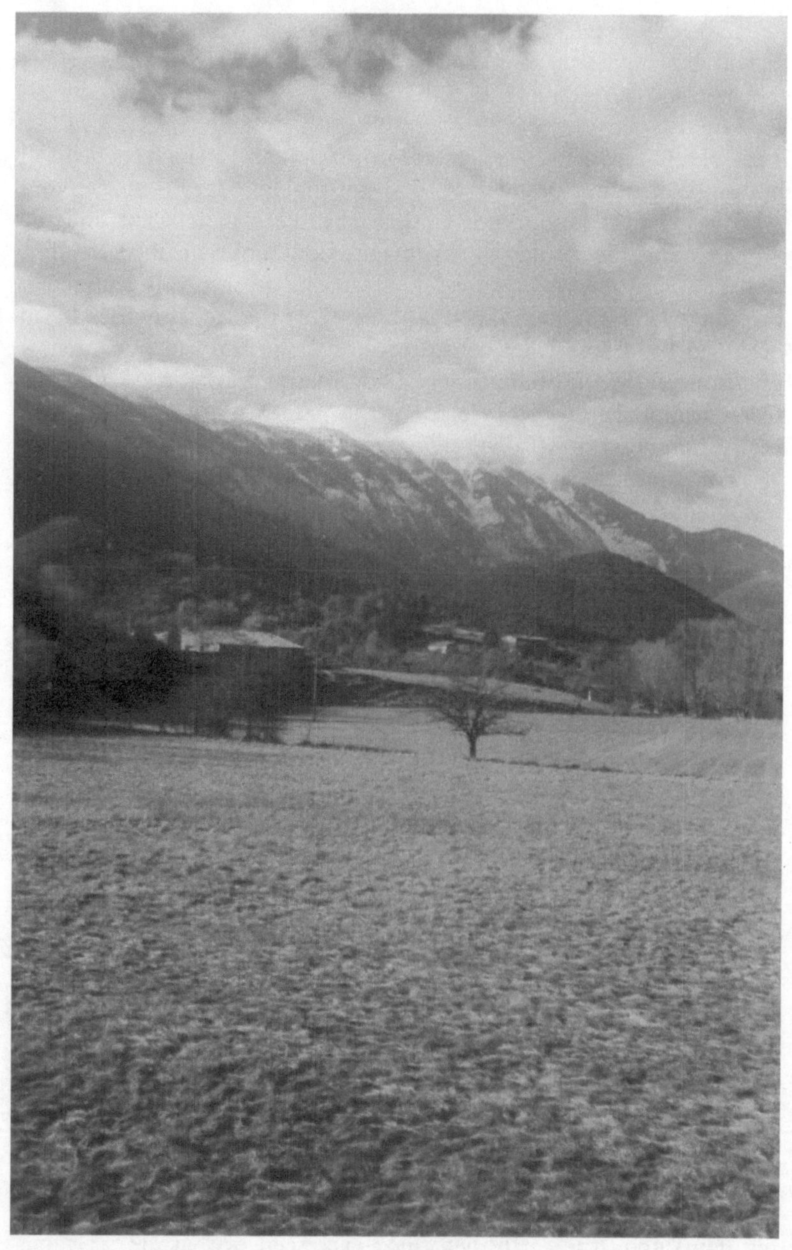

FIGURE 8. View of fields and Mont Ventoux.

chaotic irregularity is contrasted with the regularity and order that characterizes the perfection of the created world. Barren and inaccessible, the mountaintop has always been susceptible of dual interpretation: either a melancholic sign of the postlapsarian imperfection of the world and the decay of nature, or a mystical symbol of a possible rapport between humanity and the divine.[22] This explains, in great part, the divergence between different experiences of mountains, and by extension the paradox at the center of the future theory of the sublime, for which the mountain would be a key emblem. The ascent of mountains could inspire either mystic exultation or ascetic mortification, amazement and awe or aversion and terror. Thus the mountain peak could equivocally serve as the vantage point from which transcendence is accessible or the last step before the abyss. However, in Augustine's epoch, only God could be the true object of such awe: the mountain was neither experienced as sublime nor even taken as a symbol of God's greatness. Whence, for Augustine, the fate of both the imposing mountain and the welcoming garden: both are eclipsed by celestial glory in what Fitter refers to as a topography grown insubstantial and insignificant. It is what I would understand in terms of an "aesthetics of dematerialization": an iconoclastic meditation upon the formless, infinite, empty azure sky effected through a contemplation without images and dimensions, wholly appropriate as praise of an unrepresentable god—Augustine's point at which the "dreams and the visions of his imagination spoke no more." Having chosen worldly renunciation and mystical interiority, Augustine was well aware of the limitations of the world: "My soul was a burden, bruised and bleeding. It was tired of the man who carried it, but I found no place to set it down to rest. Neither the charm of the countryside nor the sweet scents of a garden could soothe it."[23] Nature is transformed into hieroglyph, analogy, symbol, allegory.

By the time of Petrarch, some of this sense of awe at the infinite and the transcendent had already been transferred to the world: the poet feels no contempt whatsoever for nature, and the glory of divine transcendence is counterbalanced by the splendors of the natural world. If Petrarch needed to make a choice atop the mountain, it was in part because the psyche of that time—the moment of transformation from the late Middle Ages to the Renaissance—could not sustain the sorts of contradictions that would later characterize the sublime, equivocating between an infinite God, infinite space, and an infinite number of worlds. This suggests that Petrarch's excision of part of the cited passage in Augustine was, if not quite an act of willful misreading, at least the symptom of an unresolvable existential contradiction typical of his epoch. Petrarch's resolution of the problem opened up a radically new way of experiencing the world. It is precisely in the passage suppressed by Petrarch ("... I have not been looking at them with my eyes ...") that the radical difference between their allegorizations of the world, of the mountain, is realized. For Augustine, the relegation of the reality of the world to memory is the sign of a mystical faith. It would appear that for Petrarch, this faith was the very destiny for which Augustine's *Confessions* served as a guide. And yet, for Petrarch, the disappearance of the mountain and its worldly panorama would function very differently, indeed antithetically. It would become the sign of destiny evaded, circumvented, reconstituted; it would imply a turn from mystic faith to a very different vision of the world. While Augustine's ascetic and mystical *contemptus mundi* caused him to reduce both garden and mountain to an allegory of that inner experience which was a sign of his love of God, Petrarch made the anchoritic mountain disappear as a pretext for a rapprochement with nature. This reconciliation with the world was effected in a site of far greater sensual possibilities, his very own, very real *hortus conclusus:* Petrarch's microcosm was the protective garden at Fontaine-de-Vaucluse, in turn symbolized by the entire Vaucluse region. The disappearance of the Ventoux established a major transformation of metaphor and allegory: no longer a sign of religious transcendence, it became a trope for psychological immanence. The public, communal, religious, universal space symbolized by the vast panorama seen from the Ventoux was abandoned for the private, local, affective space of the garden. Unlike the monks of the Middle Ages, who inhabited enclosed monestary cloisters—symbolizing the perfections of paradise—to retreat from the world, Petrarch would choose to live in both protected garden and open countryside. The disappearance of Mont Ventoux designates the end of the reign of absolute transcendence; its occlusion indicates the origin of that incipient transformation of the human spirit that will later be termed "humanism"—a new modality of thought which gave rise to an autobiography more directly centered on the self, and a poetry more closely engaged with the sensible world.

Petrarch was, in fact, well aware (or at least became retrospectively conscious), of the gravity of omitting the latter part of the citation from Augustine. In a letter to Father Francesco of the Church of the Holy Apostles dated some time after 1348, where he describes in greatest detail his two gardens, he writes of his summers spent at the source of the Sorgue in decidedly ascetic terms:

> I have declared war on my body. May He be my witness without whose assistance I would fall, for I feel that my gullet, belly, tongue, ears, and eyes often seem wicked enemies and not fitting parts of my body. Indeed I recall that many of my misfortunes occured because of them, particularly because of my eyes, which have always led me into some trouble. I have thus closed them, so that they behold barely anything but the heavens, mountains, and springs; they do not behold gold or gems, ivory or fine clothes; they do not see any horses except the two humble ones that carry me and my servant around these valleys.[24]

Yet Petrarch is being disingenuous, for clearly his eyes are not fully closed to the world. Unlike Augustine, who seals his eyes in order to relegate the world to the "vast cloisters"[25] of memory, Petrarch's eyes are but half-shut. The scene from which he turns his vision is not the entire world, but that of "gold or gems, ivory or fine clothes," that is to say, the worldly domain of Avignon, with its Roman Church in decadent exile. His eyes shut out all of the world except precisely those heavens, mountains, springs, and valleys of the Vaucluse that he so loved. Never was his misappropriation of Augustinian rhetoric for his own earthly (if not worldly, and certainly not otherworldy) ends more clearly expressed. His ascesis is writerly, not saintly.

Petrarch made Mont Ventoux disappear so as to escape from the symbolic web of the sacred mountain (biblical, Augustinian, Dantesque) which would have forced his poetic efforts into a spiritual mold. Petrarch would circumvent, indeed dissimulate, God's pneuma in persuance of his own poetic breath. Henceforth, the natural world would offer the possibility of reflecting Petrarch's own soul. The realism that permeated his account of Mont Ventoux would be transformed in his poetry, where mountains would become symbolic or emblematic, mere silhouettes decorating the emotional landscape. The Ventoux was Petrarch's sacrifice, and it would be his invisible monument, never to be visited again. His discourse on the mountain, his discourse of the mountain, his discourse against the mountain, would be the very precondition of his poetry.

The immanence Petrarch sought was not Augustine's, an undivided will replete with God. The mountain, as a sign of transcendence, needed to be replaced with another symbol, a new sign of his own immanence. When Augustine sought refuge from his madness, he found it in a garden; when he finally realized mystical union with God, it was a real garden that encompassed the heavenly, metaphysical source. "But we laid the lips of our hearts to the heavenly stream that flows from your fountain, the source of all life which is in you, so that as far as it was in our power to do so we might be sprinkled with its waters and in some sense reach an understanding of this great mystery."[26] Petrarch would seek a different garden and a different stream, a muse rather than a god: the garden would be Fontaine-de-Vaucluse, and the river the Sorgue, "ch'a pianger et cantar m'aita" (which helps me weep and sing).[27]

> Here I have acquired two small gardens perfectly suited to my skills and taste. To attempt a description for you would be too long. In short, I believe that no similar spot exists in all the world, and, to confess my unmanly fickleness, I regret only that it is not in Italy. I customarily call it my transalpine Helicon. The one garden is very shady, suitable only for study and sacred to our Apollo. It overhangs the source of the Sorgue, and beyond it lies nothing but ravines and cliffs, remote and accessible only to wild beasts or birds. The other garden, near the house, appears more cultivated, and it is a delight to Bacchus. This one, astonishing as it may seem, is in the midst of the very beautiful and swift-running river. Nearby, divided from it by a very small bridge on the further side of the house, hangs a curved vault of native rock that now provides shelter against the summer heat. It is a place that inspires studies, and I suspect is not too dissimilar to the little hall where Cicero used to declaim his orations, except that his did not have a Sorgue flowing alongside. Under this vault, therefore, I spend my afternoons, and my mornings on the hillsides; the evenings I spend in the meadows or in my less cultivated garden at the source where my efforts have conquered nature and cleared a spot under the high cliff in the midst of the waters, narrow indeed but very inspiring, in which even a sluggish mind can rise to the noblest thoughts.[28]

Rise to the noblest thoughts? It is astonishing that in this letter—which begins with Petrarch's paraphrase of Augustine about closing his eyes to the world—Petrarch celebrates the gardens, fields, and forests of the Vaucluse, allegorized as the mountain abode of the muses, the Helicon. Even more astonishing is the fact that the specific gods that reign in these regions are Bacchus and Apollo, that decidedly polytheistic opposition which would inspire European thought from the ancient Greeks through Nietzsche—a mythopoeic differentiation representing the antithetical states of intoxication and dreams, of joyful libidinal excess and beautifully organized form. Petrarch's two great inspirations had always been Augustine and Cicero, the Christian and the pagan. In honor of Augustine, Petrarch sacrificed the Ventoux, for neither memory nor true faith demand a sacred mountain. In imitation of Cicero, for whom both the natural landscape and cultivated garden were literary stimuli, Petrarch would transform the natural setting of Fontaine-de-Vaucluse into a veritable *studium,* a site of inspiration and oration, of meditation and work.[29] Indeed, most of his major works were written there, and the lay of the land, the sounds of the countryside, and the forces of the weather all animated his writing.[30] Petrarch's empathy with nature, along with his powers of observation and description (both of nature and the self), were new phenomena in European letters, now open not only to the verities of the eternal, but also to the sundry inspirations of the moment. This novel sensitivity shattered the grip that ancient rhetorical commonplaces held on poetry: now the totality of creation was available to express his inner moods and passions. The natural world became an intimate system of symbols, poetry an expression of the soul. Petrarch had inaugurated a new ratio between the sensual and the spiritual that continues to inspire poetic lyricism.

For Petrarch, the geography of the Vaucluse—specifically the natural wonder which is the rocky enclosure of the source of the Sorgue—is the very emblem of his isolation. Field, forest, hill, cliff, river, garden: Petrarch made the site his own, partially in contrast to the horrors of the city (Avignon) with its decadent multitudes, but mainly to foster the conditions necessary to the creation of poetry.[31] Petrarch was a poet of exile: from his country (Italy), his city (Avignon), his literary language (Latin), and especially from the very scene of his secret inspiration, Mont Ventoux. He sought a rootedness—in the Vaucluse, at Fontaine-de-Vaucluse, within his gardens, within his soul—that he himself invented. His rhetoric on the subject is subtle and careful. In a letter to Giovanni Colonna, he simultaneously offers a diatribe against Avignon and a celebration of the countryside, all the while proferring a hidden critique of the papal schism:

> For where outside of Italy could I find a more peaceful place? You will see me contented with the hospitality of a modest but shady and narrow garden [. . . .] You will see me from morning to night, wandering around alone, roving over the meadows and mountains and fountains, living in the woods and in the countryside, fleeing human footsteps, following the birds, loving the shadows, enjoying the mossy caves and the blooming meadows, cursing the cares of the Curia, avoiding the bustle of the cities, shunning the doors of the exalted, mocking the undertakings of the multitude, and keeping equal distance from joy and sadness; enjoying my leisure all day and night, glorying in a partnership with the Muses, amidst the sound of birds and nymphs, and accompanied by few servants but many books.[32]

The opposition beween the "curse" on the Curia and the "glorification" of the Muses is complex, containing the major oppositions operative in Petrarch's thought: Rome and Avignon, sacred Latin church and secular Italian literature, the vulgate and the vernacular, theology and poetry, city and country, society and isolation.

Every writer occupies a unique space, a specific topography, a local geography. Petrarch defined one limit of the writerly *topos:* the bucolic asceticism which was already a literary model in ancient Greece and Rome would now be seen as a precondition of writing, a source of inspiration, the very basis of writerly technique. "I mean a solitude that is not exclusive, leisure that is neither idle nor profitless but productive of advantage to many."[33] Petrarch enumerates three types of solitude: in place (such as Fontaine-de-Vaucluse), in time (such as the night), in soul (concerning the powers of concentrated contemplation), all of which are necessary for religious meditation and poetic inspiration.[34] There are two primary material necessities for a writer: silence and solitude. Very much in the tradition of pastoral retreat—whether that of patrician Romans escaping to country estates amidst a crumbling empire, anchorites mortifying body and soul in desert hermitages, or ecclesiastics choosing the monastic life—Petrarch would, like so many writers after him, castigate all those destroyers of the silence and shadow necessary for poetic inspiration. Yet silence is always composed of sound: at Fontaine-de-Vaucluse, that of rushing water, birdsong, animal cries, and the various winds, notably the mistral. And solitude is always comprised of place: the closed valley of the Vaucluse; the naturally cloistered site of Fontaine-de-Vaucluse; the green cabinet of the writer's garden; the paradoxical feeling of the body's equilibrium and excitation as inspiration makes the word appear; and the certainty that the soul, immanence incarnate, is destined to be expressed, exteriorized, metamorphized into poetry. "Mai non fui in parte ove sì chiar vedessi quel che veder vorrei . . ." (I have never been anywhere where I could see so clearly what I wish to see . . .).[35] The Vaucluse is a world apart.

The inspiration of the ancients directly and profoundly informed the creation of Petrarch's garden, as is so beautifully expressed in a letter to Cardinal Colonna:

> You have perhaps heard of my war with the Nymphs. We argue about borders; here is what it is all about. Near the source of the Sorgue arise enormous rocks on both sides of the site, open to the winds and the clouds; fountains flow from the feet of these boulders, and it is there that the Nymphs reign. The Sorgue originates in a cave and with great tumult rolls its fresh and icy waters upon a bed carpeted with pebbles resembling emeralds.
>
> I possess a small rocky field in the middle of these waters, where I attempt to lodge those Muses who are chased away from everywhere else. This is the reason for the great war with the Nymphs. They find it inappropriate that I want to put strangers in their place, and that I prefer nine old maids to a thousand young virgins.
>
> By dint of moving stones, I finally managed to form a little meadow that was beginning to become green, but a band of furious Nymphs impetuously descended from the rocks and destroyed my burgeoning meadow. Frightened by this sudden irruption, I climbed up onto the rocks to observe the damage they caused. The storm passed, and I descended, ashamed of my flight, to return things to their previous state. Yet hardly had the sun encircled the globe, but the Nymphs returned to battle, overturning everything and moving in to occupy our caves.[36]

It would be an error to take Petrarch's nymphs and naiades, muses and dryads, Greek and Roman gods and goddesses, as mere metaphors. The Sorgue is his muse, and Petrarch himself is the new *genius loci* of the Sorgue. He makes the river speak.[37] It is true, however, that although he mentions that the source of the Sorgue is supremely worthy of an altar, he qualifies his words: "Such altars, Christ is my witness, I have long thought of erecting, if opportunity should favor my wishes, there in my little garden which lies in the shadow of the cliffs and overhangs the stream, and I shall dedicate them not to the nymphs, as Seneca thought, nor to any of the pagan deities of springs and rivers, but to Mary, whose ineffable conception and fruitful virginity overturned all the altars and temples of the gods."[38] Petrarch sought a delicate balance between the sacred and the profane, between the empirical and the spiritual. This balance, it should be noted, was always at stake in all but the most ascetic examples of Christian theology: the conciliation between the empirical and the anagogic was, from the early Church fathers through the Middle Ages, a crucial aspect of Christian writing, to the point that the very rhetorical structure of a theologian such as Ambrose, for example, was deeply influenced by the rhetoric and poetry of Virgil (as was Petrarch). Indeed, extreme mystical renunciation was almost always tempered by the counterpart of a mysticism that had direct roots in the sensual natural world, such as that of the Franciscan order, and even more so by the sort of empirical utilitarianism of the Cistercians, for whom the productive husbandry of the land was deemed a blessing.[39] The psychological drama of Petrarch's existence—unlike that of Augustine, for whom the pagan, Manichaen temptation was all too real—was not theologically, but poetically and erotically, motivated. Augustine's peace with God, and with himself, came through mystical union, obviating further passion for the natural world; his ascent towards transcendence was absolute. Petrarch, to the contrary, renounced such mystical ascent, just as he sacrificed the Ventoux and what it would have meant according to the ancient symbolism. Rather than abolish all contradictions, both inner and outer, he would nurture them as the very origins of his inspiration, by reconciling the sensual and the spiritual.

As Petrarch's rhetoric was articulated by a delicate balance between the Rome of the Church and the Rome of the ancient poets, his inspiration derived from two very different sources: his passion for the Vaucluse countryside that contained the natural "source" of his inspiration, the source of the Sorgue; and his love, however chaste, of a woman, Laura, who was to become the object of much of his poetry. His genius was to articulate these two loves, to make each the metaphor of the other—as did the troubadors before him, intimately linking the pleasures of the landscape to feelings of secular passion—converting their union into the metaphor of his soul.[40] The manner in which he affectively personalized topography, merging landscape and mindscape, established a new ratio between sensuality and spirituality in European poetry: immanence might still be the site of lasting faith, but it was also, and perhaps more so, the place of an immediate, sensual joy that owed little to religion. And whatever debt he owed to the troubadors' spiritualization of love, Petrarch eschewed both the conventions and formalities of the courtly sensibility and the use of that rich tradition of commonplace motifs which abound in their poetry. While for the troubadors individual poetic voice was in part a function of the rhetorical manipulation of such clichés, Petrarch's individuality would appear both rhetorically and psychologically. Consider one example among so many, the final two stanzas of one of his *Rima Sparse,* where the author, amidst the hills of the Vaucluse, laments the death of his beloved Laura:

> Non è sterpo né sasso in questi monti,
> non ramo o fronda verde in queste piagge,
> non fiore in queste valli o foglia d'erba,
>
> stilla d'acqua non ven di queste fonti,
> né fiere àn questi boschi sì selvagge,
> che non sappian quanto è mia pena acerba.[41]
>
> [No shrub or stone in these mountains,
> no branch or green leaf on these slopes,
> no flower in these valleys nor blade of grass,
>
> no trickle of water comes from these springs,
> nor do these woods have beasts so savage,
> that they do not know how bitter is my sorrow.]

For Saint Francis, the love of the world's beauty went far beyond the aesthetic; in Fitter's words, "armed with holiness, he acted out the pathetic fallacy. Just as in pastoral beasts and trees are said to mourn or celebrate the fortunes of individuals, so the flora and fauna of Italy are accredited by Francis with active powers of responsive sympathy."[42] Indeed, the very mystery of the Redemption is symbolized by a mystical landscape which darkened and trembled at the moment of Christ's death, as if in wrath and mourning. In Petrarch's poetry, the "pathetic fallacy"—the ascription of human traits or feelings to nature—is truly the expression of pathos, and never a fallacy. And yet, how powerful can such a resonance with nature be? What would it mean to identify with, to be one with, the Ventoux or the mistral? Might this not lead to madness, poetic or otherwise?

In 1333 Petrarch abandoned Avignon, disgusted by the city and its culture. In 1336 he climbed Mont Ventoux, the moment of his great renunciation of his passion for Laura: as he wrote in that famous letter, "What I used to love I no longer love."[43] His ascent was sublimation in both senses of the word: the *spiritual* sublimation of vision into faith, and the *erotic* sublimation of passion into poetry. In 1337 he bought his property at Fontaine-de-Vaucluse, began his gardens, and fathered a child out of wedlock, perhaps a sign that his love for Laura was indeed over, now set at a distance, transformed, interiorized, sublimated, ripe for poetry. In 1341 he was crowned poet laureate in Rome. In a certain sense, Petrarch indeed managed to reach the summit by descending: from the mountain to the garden, from the heavens to the source. In 1347 he left Provence to live in Italy. Laura died in 1348. Petrarch died in 1374. After his letter of 1336, he never again mentioned Mont Ventoux. However, in *Secretum* he wrote: "As often as you behold at sunset the shadows of the mountains lengthening on the plain, say to yourself: 'Now life is sinking fast; the shadow of death begins to overspread the scene; yonder sun tomorrow will again be rising the same, but this day of mine will never come back.'"[44] Can we wonder which mountain he had in mind?

II

Disappearance

> The void attracts: it isolates our personality, it places us at the center of the universe.
>
> —Alberto Savinio, *Dico a te, Clio*

In 1992, immediately after the publication in Paris of my Mirrors of Infinity: The French Formal Garden and 17th-Century Metaphysics, *I was invited to appear on Alain Veinstein's radio broadcast dedicated to recent publications,* Du jour au lendemain. *At the end of the interview, he posed a question—in the form of a play on words—intended to lead me into some revelations more intimate than those allowed in the mostly philosphical discussion that preceded. He asked, "Avez-vous un jardin secret?" (Have you a secret garden?), that is, a hidden part of your life. Taking the question literally, I answered no. "Not even in childhood?," he insisted. Giving in, I answered, "Have you seen Resnais's film* Mon oncle d'Amérique*?" "Yes." "Do you remember the last scene?" "Yes." "There is a long shot of a desolate urban landscape in ruins. Then a medium shot of a wall covered with graffiti. Finally a closeup of that wall, revealing graffiti and lichen forming an abstract pattern. That's my secret garden. That's where I was born. The South Bronx."*

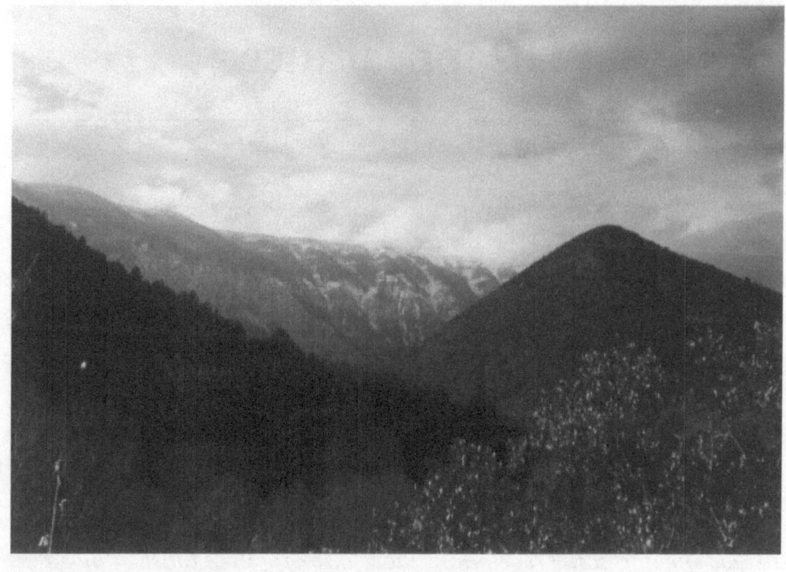

FIGURE 9. The peaks of Mont Ventoux.

For half a millenium after Petrarch wrote the letter commonly referred to as "The Ascent of Mont Ventoux"—which has long been deemed a classic text demarcating the origins of Renaissance humanism—not a word had been written about this mountain in poetry or literature, hardly a painting created depicting this most impressive of Provençal sites.[1] What can explain these five hundred years of silence? How was the mountain transformed from forbidding to forbidden? I believe that it did not occur simply because Petrarch's depiction of the Ventoux was so brilliant, unique, unsurpassable; nor because it was an unrepeatable origin of an incipient humanism; nor even because a certain anxiety of influence blocked such an enticing path for the renovation of our poetry, psychology, and philosophy. No, I believe that it was Petrarch's disavowal, his abnegation of the Ventoux, his absolute insistence on the Ventoux's disappearance, his veritable annihilation of the mountain, that for centuries hindered its representation. I believe that the shepherd's words were premonitory. The centuries of silence were in imitation of disappearance, mimetic of nothingness. Or perhaps, to be more precise, I should speak of Mont Ventoux's self-effacement, and suggest that it was the mountain itself that went into hiding.

It should be noted that when Petrarch describes his nearly ecstatic vision of the landscape from the peak of Mont Ventoux, he speaks of what he sees in every direction except the north, the mythic bearing that symbolizes all that is bleak, wintery, desolate, pernicious. Indeed, the land of predilection for Petrarch was precisely what was visible to the south, east, and west: that is, the region approximately congruous with modern day Provence and Languedoc, the lands south of the Loire where traditionally the Provençal and Languedocian dialects are spoken.[2] The north, that is, the other half of modern day France, was almost nonexistent for him. Petrarch took only one trip north in his life, a journey of which he never wrote, neither in his biographical works nor in his vast correspondence. In a letter to Neri Morandi, he explains: "I do not like those Caesars who come to us from the North: everything is icy in those climates; there, hearts are not warmed by that noble flame which causes the heart to rise and which I sense as the vital heat of the empire. It would be better for us if our emperors came from the land of the setting sun, or from the South.

Nothing is worse than the North."[3] Petrarch far preferred the sensual Mediterranean sensibility to that of the cerebral Hyperborean regions. From the point of view of Petrarch's chosen home in Fontaine-de-Vaucluse, the Ventoux existed at the limits of his world. The question of limits and borders—cultural, natural, and supernatural—was crucial. In the transition from the symbolic art of the Middle Ages to the realism of the Renaissance, the first instances of precise realist representation took place in the margins of manuscripts, those empty places that permitted nonsymbolic decoration and precise depiction. Freedom of creativity existed in the margins. Petrarch, for example, inscribed many of the margins of the books in his library with autobiographical notes, placing the facts of his life alongside the poetry, rhetoric, and theology of others. Mont Ventoux was Petrarch's north. Mont Ventoux was the margin that permitted his new sensibility to flourish. Mont Ventoux was Petrarch's major marginalia.

Consider this other description of the view from the peak of Mont Ventoux in *Calendau* [Calendal], an epic poem written in Provençal and published in 1866 by Frédéric Mistral, the great Provençal writer who bore the name of that persistent, horrible, unearthly northerly wind known to drive both animals and humans mad:

Entre tant de colo ounte sauto
Nosto Prouvènço, la plus auto
Belèu es lou Ventour : vesès, d'eilamoundaut,
Li mountagnolo Dóufinenco,
E Coumtadino e Gardounenco,
Talo que d'erso peirounenco,
E lou Rose menu coume un fiéu argentau.

De l'Auro, lou Ventour esfraio :
Coume dirian uno muraio
Se drèisso, fieramen taia de cap à pèd ;
Negro courouno de verduro,
Un bos de mèle, ligno duro,
Èro la machicouladuro
Dóu bàrri fourmidable, e pourtavo respèt.[4]

[Between so many mountains arises
Our Provence, the highest

Perhaps is the Ventoux: from the summit are seen,
    The mountains of the Dauphiné,
    The Comtat and the Gard,
    Like petrified waves,
And the Rhone thin as a silver thread.

    From the North, the Ventoux is frightening:
    One would say like a wall
It arises, grandly chiseled from foot to peak;
    A black crown of trees,
    A forest of larch, a hard line,
    Serves as the machicoulis
And the portal of the formidable rampart.]

It should be noted that while in this context the term *"l'Auro"* signifies the north, its prime meaning is that of the north wind—a subtle identification of Mont Ventoux with the wind that seems to be part of its very essence, the wind that names its peak, the Col des Tempêtes. It is not the view towards the north—the view of a France not Provençal, the view of the Gallic other that ultimately conquered Provence—that is decribed, but rather the terrifying north slope itself. The omission of a northern vista was certainly a most conscious aesthetic and political act, since for Mistral, the most famous author of the Felibrige movement (founded in 1854 to valorize Provençal culture, demarcated from the rest of French letters), the North was anathema.

A major aspect of Petrarch's humanism is that he wrote most of his poetry in a vernacular language, Italian, inspired by the Provençal poetry of the troubadors, who sang the lands and the loves of Provence. This was yet another manner of escaping the influence of the Latin Church on his poetry. But this means that Petrarch didn't sing the Ventoux in its native tongue. Might it be that Mont Ventoux awaited the renascence of the Provençal language and its poetry to appear again? Might it be that certain sites can only be expressed in their native tongue? What more impressive monument to Provence and Provençal culture than Mont Ventoux?

In his *Memòri e raconti* [Memoires and Tales], Mistral again describes the view from the peak of Mont Ventoux, recounting the ascent of September 1857, when he was accompanied by the poet

Théodore Aubanel and the painter Pierre Grivolas: "We saw the sun surge forth like a superb king of glory from between the brilliant peaks of the snow-covered Alps, and the shadow of the Ventoux grow and lengthen throughout the entirety of the Comtat Venaissin, and beyond, upon the Rhone and well into the Languedoc, the triangulation of its immense cone."[5] Again, the view to the north is not mentioned; again, the north slope itself is described as "harsh and extremely steep."[6] In this account, after Mistral and his traveling companions descend the mountain and continue their hike towards the town of Sault, they encounter an old man who asks what they were up to, taking them for collectors of medicinal herbs. They respond that they had just come from Mont Ventoux. The old man—echoing the words of the shepherd Petrarch had encountered just before his own ascent—replies sententiously: "Wise is he who does not return there, but mad is he who does!"[7]

Mont Ventoux is simultaneously the core of Provence and the antithesis of Provence. It is hyperbolic in all respects: eminently visible from nearly all parts of Provence, it is the highest point in the region, with its summit at 1912 meters; its peak, the appropriately named Col des Tempêtes, is perpetually buffeted by the wind, which in February 1967 gusted to 320 kilometers per hour, a world record; the visibility from its peak, as we have already seen in several accounts, is legendary; and, of particular interest for our study, it has been described in terms of the greatest austerity—the "bald mountain of Provence"—and has been compared to a "pile of rocks broken for road repair."[8] What it shares with other bald mountains is its diabolical nature: the north slope is so forbidding and terrifying that some believe one of its caves, the Baume de Méne, is among the entrances to hell. This is hardly the beloved Provence that has long spawned best-selling travel guides and idyllic accounts of a year's sojourn or a house reconstructed; the Provence of sunshine and olive groves, honey and wild thyme, vineyards and lavender fields. Paradoxically, Mont Ventoux represents, at the very core of Provence, a warning against tourism and development, against modernization and appropriation. The Ventoux is an anti-Provence.

The majestic stature and fierce emptiness of this grim mountain inspires violence. The eighteenth century saw a transformation of the experience of the physical terror and metaphysical vertigo known as the sublime. The theory of the sublime was first expounded by the philosopher Longinus at the dawn of the Christian era: It was then effectively analyzed by Thomas Burnet in *The Sacred Theory of the Earth* (1684), later integrated into the writings of the Earl of Shaftesbury, then differentiated from the notion of beauty in Joseph Addison's *Pleasures of the Imagination* (1712), and finally systematized by Edmund Burke in *A Philosophical Enquiry into the Origin of Our Ideas of the Sublime and the Beautiful* (1757). Burke defines the sublime as the strongest emotion of which the mind is capable, an astonishment and amazement that shocks the soul, a sort of terror.[9] Its twofold cause is essentially the *hyperbolic* (obscurity, power, vastness, infinity, magnificence), and the *privative* (vacuity, darkness, solitude, silence). It is curious that the latter conditions for this most extreme emotional and metaphysical state correspond to the exceedingly intimate and quiescent conditions that are valued by so many writers. This is perhaps one reason why the sublime was so attractive to the romantic sensibility: it not only synthesized the antithetical conditions of plenitude and privation, but it also, paradoxically, coalesced the material conditions necessary for writing with those that hinder the creative act.

Marjorie Hope Nicolson, in *Mountain Gloom and Mountain Glory,* characterizes the sublime in terms of an "aesthetics of the infinite": "Awe, compounded of mingled terror and exultation, once reserved for God, passed over in the seventeenth century first to an expanded cosmos, then from the macrocosm to the greatest objects in the geocosm—mountains, ocean, desert."[10] It is as if the history of the sublime suffered a declension from deity to cosmos to earth, to finally end as a psychological syndrome in Kant's *Critique of Judgment.* Each epoch manifests a need to mediate the incommensurable, to grasp infinity and eternity, to express the unattainable goals of the imagination: the infinite plenitude of the godhead (Plotinus) was bridged by mystical ecstasy; the infinite emptiness of the cosmic spaces (Pascal) was investigated through fictive cosmic voyages (inspired by Newton's discoveries); the vast Alpine mountains were explored during the excursions of the romantics. With the progressive materialization of the objects of the sublime came increased description and depiction of those objects, notably mountains. The complex and contradictory feelings aroused by mountains is wonderfully expressed by John Dennis, whose account of his 1688 traversal of the

Alps was to become a *locus classicus* of the link between mountains and the sublime: what he felt was expressed in terms of oxymorons, "a delightful Horrour, a terrible Joy."[11] The mountain can be the source of either torment or bliss, the site of either ascesis or ecstasy—or both at once. We find here a succinct expression of the conflict that will mark modern aesthetics, the questions as to whether the sublime is distinct from beauty or the consummation of beauty; whether the sublime is to be a rhetorical, theological, natural, ontological, or psychological principle; whether the experience of the sublime damages or improves the soul. However, as has always been the case, while philosphers attempt to resolve paradoxes, poets prefer to transform them into the dynamic core of their work.

Immanuel Kant expanded on these principles in his "Analytic of the Sublime" in the *Critique of Judgment* (1790), postulating a realm of the "dynamically sublime in nature"—a sort of *natura naturans,* nature as active principle—where the might and terror inspired by nature is epitomized by formations and events that portend the infinite, beyond the scope of human comprehension. Among those things that evoke the sublime are "bold, overhanging, and as it were threatening rocks."[12] The precipitous, rocky crags of the highest mountains, and more specifically the summits of the Alps, would become the romantic emblem of the sublime, evoking vast emptiness, blinding light, translucid atmosphere, olympian heights, archaic peaks, terrifying chasms, majestic glaciers. Such is a poetics of adjectival hyperbole, where the nominal is never sufficiently substantial. However, even though the north slope of the Ventoux certainly bears all the characteristics needed to evoke these most awe-inspiring feelings, this harshest and most mysterious of Provençal mountains is never invoked in the discourse of the sublime, neither by the romantics who would have been expected to take note of such a strange natural formation, nor by those regionalists who should have sung its praises, nor even by those urban aestheticians, critics, and painters who sought the limits of artistic expression.

The modern, if not modernist, mythologization of Mont Ventoux is inaugurated by Mistral's *Calendau,* a poetic epic whose hero, Calendau, engages in a series of herculean efforts to win the hand of his beloved, Esterello, also courted by the evil Comte Severan.[13] The seventh song is a strange hymn, or rather antihymn, to Mont Ventoux. Here, our hero makes the rugged ascent, ever fearful of tumbling into the terrifying abyss, in order to make his fortune by cutting down the "bewitched forest"[14] of larch that crowns its peak, those "superb giants, ancient solitaries which, through an involuntary fear, afflict the heart, oh! excuse me! and salvation!"[15] Calendau would write this tale with his axe.[16] As he stood, admiring these fabulous, grandiose trees,

> La Ventoureso matiniero,
> En trespirant dins la sourniero
> Dis aubre, fernissié coume un pur cantadis . . .[17]
>
> [The morning northeast wind,
> Breathing in the obscurity
> Of the trees, trembled like a pure cantata . . .]

But, once the battle began, once iron struck wood, the sounds were suddenly and inexorably transformed:

> Tout-en-un-cop l'aubre cracino :
> Dóu cabassòu à la racino
> Gemis de branco en branco un sourne rangoulun,
> E de soun trone, dins la coumbo,
> L'aubre de-tèsto-pouncho toumbo . . .
> Pereilavau, es uno troumbo
> Que trono, e reboumbis en un long tremoulun.[18]
>
> [All of a sudden the tree cracked:
> From crown to root
> Groaning from branch to branch with a somber death-rattle
> And from its throne, in the valley,
> The tree fell headfirst . . .
> Into the depths, like a waterspout,
> That thunders, and rebounds in a long tremor.]

The gentle, melodious assonance of the breeze—La Ventoureso, named after the mountain, or perhaps vice versa—was obliterated by the harsh, crashing consonants of the falling trees. For nine days the mountain resounded with the effects of Calendau's superhuman effort, as each and every tree attacked repeated the plaint of the first. The forest fell like a deluge, and it was as if Mont Ventoux itself were crashing down.[19] The work was finished; the song of the forest silenced, the mountain shorn. Once again the Ventoux practically disappeared, as Calendau sacrificed it for his love. Proud of his work, he bragged of his efforts to Esterello, who responded with scorn: "You have dishonored the face of the Ventoux!"[20] She insisted—echoing the thoughts of Augustine, Petrarch, and so many others—that even if the plains, the chestnut trees, and the olive groves belong to man, "the mountains, the supercillious peaks, belong to God!"[21] But perhaps Calendau knew better, for already at the moment that he made his initial ascent in total silence and solitude, at the risk of his life, he sensed that whatever he would do could not dishonor the mountain, for its curse was more primal than any human deed: "Es de lio mounte Diéu n'a passa que de-nieu" (God only came to this mountain at night). The French translation of this sentence (in the volume cited herein) is: "Lieux sinistres, où Dieu ne passa que de nuit!" (A sinister place, where God came only by night).[22] In Provençal (as in French), the effect of the *passé composé,* the past perfect tense *(a passa)*—which maintains a sense of continuity with the present—is that the mountain is indeed sinister, since God only appears at night. In the French translation, the replacement of the *passé composé* by the *passé simple,* the literary preterit tense *(passa)* is, in the context, astonishing and emblematic. It suggests a completed action in a bygone era—relegated to a historic, mythic, or fairy-tale past—indicating that perhaps God no longer appears there at all. The explicit addition of *lieux sinistres* (sinister places) is quite superfluous. This transposition of tenses might well imply a profound difference between the French and the Provençal attitudes towards the Ventoux. A mountain from which God has definitively withdrawn, a mountain violently desacralized, is positively uncanny for the French. But a mountain still visited by God, even if only at night, remains a sacred, though very strange and accursed, place: Calandau's machismo would be positively sacrilegious for the Provençal sensibility, while merely historical, mythic, or literary for the French. In either case, the Ventoux is thus doubly ravaged: anathemized by God, defaced by man.

In every place is hidden an absent place. Perhaps this absence is what we call an origin. In any case, it is the source of symbols, which permits us to recall, evoke, indicate one site in the place of another. However, not all places can be symbolized: there exist rare sites that resist metaphorization, that defy mention, that avoid description, that eschew representation—sites meant to evoke an unsayable absolute. Mont Ventoux is one such place, whence five hundred years of silence on its account.

From 1867 through 1870, Stéphane Mallarmé lived in Avignon, where he met most of the major Felibres. It is said, and widely believed, that at that time the poet Théodore Aubanel and the painter Pierre Grivolas took him on an excursion to Mont Ventoux. However, the work of Mallarmé offers no mention whatsoever of this visit: neither his poetry, essays, nor correspondence bear any trace of the Ventoux which, even if not ascended, was ever present on the horizon.[23] Might the natural wonder of the Ventoux simply have been ignored? Or was this barren mass so present, so awe-inspiring, that it touched something unfathomable and inexpressible in Mallarme's soul?

By the time of his arrival in Avignon, Mallarmé had already overcome the influence of Baudelaire that had weighed so heavily on his poetry to that point. This poetic liberation was contemporaneous with a period of mental breakdown and spiritual crisis. In April 1866, Mallarmé plunged into the abyss. He wrote to Aubanel on 16 July 1866 of the certainty that he had discovered the secret to his life work: "I am dead, and resuscitated with the bejeweled key to my last spiritual Casket."[24] Writing on 14 May 1867 to Henri Cazalis, he suggests both the spiritual delicacy and the metaphysical megalomania of that condition: "I admit, furthermore, but only to you, that I still need, so great was the damage to my triumph, to look at myself in this mirror in order to think, and that if it were not in front of the table where I write this letter to you, I would once again become Nothingness. This is to let you know that I am now impersonal, and no longer the Stéphane that you knew—but rather an aptitude that the Spiritual Universe has to see itself and to develop, through what used to be me."[25] This quasi-Hegelian, solipsistic explanation received its poetic representation in four prose poems concerning "the spiritual conception of Nothingness," as well as most notably in the "Ouverture ancienne d'Hérodiade."[26] At the moment of his revelation, Mallarmé, henceforth inextricably linked to the Void, writes: "Unfortunately, while excavating verse to this point, I have encountered two abysses, which drive me to despair. One is Nothingness [. . .] the other void I found is that of my chest."[27] His crisis would now serve as inspiration rather than blockage—"for I experience moments akin to the madness glimpsed in equilibrating ecstasy"[28]—attested to by the fact that soon after the crisis he conceived of entitling one of his books either *Allégories somptueuses du Néant* or *Somptuosité du Néant.*[29]

Soon after his return to Paris, Mallarmé completed his obscure prose poem *Igitur:* an indication of his psychic recovery, an expression of his poetic liberation, a celebration of his conquest of the void, a defiance of the Absolute. In *Igitur,* Mallarmé had chosen a poetic topos already inhabited by the spirit of Edgar Allan Poe, his other major influence along with Baudelaire: not the lucid solitude and sublime terror of the mountaintop, but isolation and fear in a dark room and somber staircase at midnight, extinguished candles and vague whispers, thoughts of ashes and tombs, shadows and fantoms, suicide and nothingness. In this dream of the quest for the Absolute, he chose, as the scene of inspiration and poetic madness, an interior void rather than an exterior one, a Parisian apartment rather than a mountaintop. The tale concludes with the line: "Le Néant parti, reste le château de la pureté." (With Nothingness gone, there remains the chateau of purity.)[30] Igitur's "philosophical suicide" is tantamount to a poetic resurrection, which might well be explained by a remark Mallarmé made in a letter of 24 September 1867 to Villiers de l'Isle-Adam: ". . . to maintain an uneffacable notion of pure Nothingness *[Néant],* I needed to impose a sensation of absolute emptiness *[vide]* upon my brain."[31] Certain of Mallarmé's early poems correspond to his psychological and poetic fall into the Void, and are of particular interest concerning meditations on landscape. Jean-Pierre Richard, in *L'univers imaginaire de Mallarmé,* explains the implications of Mallarmé's conquest of the void for landscape poetry: "This invasion of nothingness also informs the landscape. Hollowed out, denuded, here the azure almost dies from an excess of azure, from a sickness of whiteness. On the other side, the earth retracts, and is summed up as 'a thin, pale line.' [. . .] The *line* thus constitutes the ultimate perceptible guarantee, the last frontier between being and non-being [. . .] between our world and the other world. . . ."[32] The landscape is essentially reduced to the horizon line, articulating earth and sky, connecting terrestrial solidity with celestial evanescence. The volatilized sky seems to vaporize the earth, the mountain is sublimed into sky, and the landscape rarefied to a line on the page.[33] Perhaps this was the fate of the Ventoux before Mallarmé's eyes.

Might there have existed for Mallarmé a profound, secret connection—not unlike the underground passage believed to exist between the Ventoux and the source of the Sorgue—between Igitur's

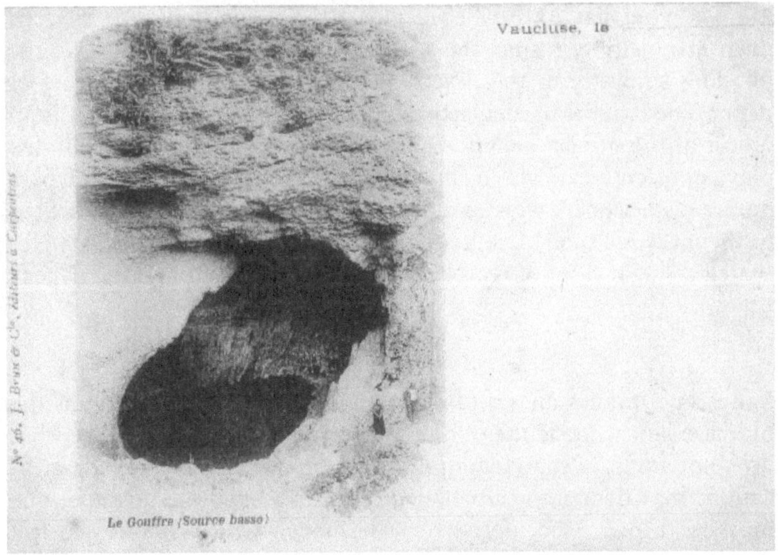

FIGURE 10. Fontaine-de-Vaucluse: The source.

gloomy interior and the vastness of the Ventoux, that *tabula rasa* of the purest, starkest whiteness? Might not the form of this void be the space of writing, the space of death: an empty room, a blank sheet of paper, terrifying whiteness? We know that Mallarmé received a copy of Mistral's recently published *Calendau,* for in a letter to the author he praises the book, explaining that for a whole month he plans to, "travel through the pines, so as to set ablaze those black solitaries of the buzzing gold of your verse, still more bee than cicada."[34] It is astonishing that even the exceedingly understated Mallarmé speaks of the forests of the Ventoux with truly untypical violence, adding his own incendiary ravages to the destruction wreaked by Calendau's axe. However, it is not at all surprising that somewhat later, Mallarmé uses the classic metaphors of ascent and descent regarding his relation to the Absolute to describe the resolution of his intense crisis: "Decidedly, I redescend from the Absolute, and I will not make of it, following Villiers' beautiful sentence, 'Poetry,' nor will I unfold, 'the living Panorama of the forms of Becoming. . . .'"[35] The panorama visible from the heights is abolished; having touched the absolute, Mallarmé rejects all such visions for his art.

The void has its privileged poetic representations: the silvered mirror, the empty frame, the still lake, the moonless night sky, the blinding snowstorm, the desert, the sea, the blank white sheet of paper. The latter is particularly treacherous for the writer. Yet it is an object of the utmost beauty. One of the most stunning museum displays in recent years was a small exhibition in New York City where numerous designers were asked to choose an object that represented to them the epitome of contemporary design. In one vitrine was presented a single sheet of recycled white 8½-by-11-inch writing paper.

Landscape implies an act of passage, a rite of passage. Perhaps the ultimate landscape is the one that always maintains a distance, that does not admit of representation, that resists rhetorical transmogrification, that demands perpetual journey. To have a landscape, one must be dispossessed, uprooted. The French word *dépaysé*—to feel strange, to be at a loss, literally to be "unlanded"—well expresses this condition. For a landscape to exist in the aesthetic sense of the term, there must be a distance from material need, from technical concerns. "Landscape" is an urban idea, where nature is abstracted from its instrumental and quotidian necessities to become an object of aesthetic contemplation. This is why it is said that the notion of landscape does not exist for peasants, whose rootedness in the earth entails primarily pragmatic concerns; this also explains why the shepherd who warned Petrarch away from the Ventoux deemed such an ascent useless.[36] The aesthetic is the strange, the estranged, the derealized, the defamiliarized, and as such it is intimately linked to the sacred, as well as to the erotic.

There exists a geography of asceticism and mysticism, as well as a geography of poetry and allegory. There also exists a geography of science. All three are linked. Writing of Ezra Pound's 1912 journey through southern France to discover the landscapes of the troubadors, Richard Sieburth delineates two major modes of nineteenth-century travel writing: "on the one hand, the 'voyage of sentiment' (in which the *dépaysement* of foreign parts serves as a stimulus to 'strange and exquisite emotions'), and on the other hand, the 'realist' method of presentation, based on the 'scientific' registering of observed fact and sensation."[37] While Pound—wishing to eliminate the sentimental for the sake of the factual in what would become his archetypically modernist "Imagist" poetry—felt these to be diametrically opposed, the sentimental and the scientific have always been combined in travel and nature writing. This is most evident in the nineteenth century, when scientific method (not always as positivist as has often been argued) became a major cognitive paradigm, producing such masterpieces as Jean-Henri Fabre's monumental *Souvenirs entomologiques* [Entomological Memoirs]. Fabre, who lived amongst the Felibres in Avignon and shared their passion for Provence, showed how the precise presentation of fact could indeed produce the most strange and exquisite emotions, and how the nonhuman worlds of plants and animals could afford the most extreme *dépaysement.*

In 1865 Fabre made his twenty-third ascent of Mont Ventoux. His remembrance of this journey reveals the beauties of the scientific spirit of observation. The plan was for their guide to take the pack animals with the group's baggage up to the Jas du Bâtiment, a small stone shelter situated at an altitude of 1550 meters. There they would await the rest of the group, which would climb to the summit to view the sunset; afterwards, they would all meet at the hut to spend the night. The group reached the peak: "To the south unfolded, as far as the eye could see, the relatively gentle slopes that we had just climbed; to the north, the scene was of a wild grandeur: the mountain, in places cut sheer down, in other places layered in a frightening declivity, is hardly but a single precipice a kilometer and a half in height."[38] The north slope is described neither in terms of mythic fables nor of the aesthetic sublime, but simply as a natural formation. The real danger of this slope is apparent, but it also serves a specific dramatic function for Fabre, as a distraction from a very different menace to come. For Fabre the writer, the north might well have held mythical or mystical force, bearing great poetic and dramatic impact; for Fabre the scientist, it functioned like the other points of the compass, as a geographic marker. All of a sudden, the peak was shrouded in a thick, rainy fog, a veritable whirlwind of a cloud in which the climbers could see no further than a foot or two in any direction. *The Ventoux disappeared before their very eyes:* not as the result of a theological revelation, as happened to Petrarch; not in an act of passionate violence, as was the case for Calandau; not out of an anxiety of influence, as might have occurred to Mallarmé; but simply in the clouds and fog and rain that cover its brilliant peak for the greater part of each year. What to do? Some thought it best to await the end of the storm, while others feared that it might continue so long that they would all be frozen in place during the night. Best to try and descend to the shelter. They all linked hands to form a human chain so that nobody would be lost, and, soaked to the skin, they tried to find the return path. But like a person blindfolded and turned around in place, they were soon totally disoriented, all points of the compass lost. How to find the south slope? How not to tumble into the northern precipice? Fabre remembered that the cloud bank had originally come from the south, but there was no guarantee that the direction of the storm hadn't changed, so it was no use following the wind. An idea: if the wind hadn't changed direction, they would be mainly soaked on one side, the one against which the wind struck for the time they hadn't lost their orientation. This was indeed the case, so they risked walking, blind, against the wind, in order to descend the safe south slope. Indeed, rather than the abyss, they found solid earth, and after twenty hesitating steps they arrived at the limit of the forest that encircled the mountaintop. But now, how to find the hut in total darkness? They were saved by their botanical knowledge and the scientific spirit of deduction, since Fabre remembered that there are two plants familiar to the Ventoux that typically grow near human habitations, the Chénopode Bon Henri (chenopodium) and the Ortie dioïque (dioecious nettle). They would only need to follow the trail of these plants towards the hut. Despite the skepticism of the others, the two believers in this system flailed about with their hands, and each sting of the nettle brought them closer to safety. Soon afterwards, they arrived at the hut. The group was saved by their knowledge of the winds and plants of Mont Ventoux.

After a hot dinner and a short sleep, the group arose at two in the morning, wishing to climb the peak again to see the sun rise. The rain had stopped and the sky promised a fine day. For some climbers—and many writers—an ascent holds the promise of spiritual rarefaction and mystical sublimation; for others, the effects are very different, very physical. Several of the participants experienced a certain nausea during the climb, for as Fabre explains, the rarified air (with the barometer at 140 ml.) is one-fifth less dense than air at sea level, thus less rich in oxygen; in their state of fatigue from the adventures of the previous day, the difference was appreciable. An ascent has physical as well as metaphysical effects: science is interested in the former, poetry in both. The climbers finally arrived to witness a stupendous sunrise:

> The Ventoux projected, to the extreme limits of the horizon, its triangular shadow, whose sides were of a slightly iridescent violet color due to the effects of the refracted light. To the south and west stretched out foggy plains where, when the sun will be higher, we will be able to see the Rhone, like a silver thread. To the north and the east was spread out, at our very feet, an enormous bank of clouds, a sort of ocean of white cotton from which there emerged, like isles of slag, the summits of lower mountains. Several peaks, with their streaks of glaciers, shone forth from the Alps.[39]

For Fabre, the scientific spirit of exact observation is intimately linked to the literary pleasures inherent in describing the natural world. Compare the nearly contemporary description by Henry David Thoreau, who journeyed in 1846 from Concord, Massachusetts, to Bangor, Maine, in order to embark upon an expedition to climb Mount Ktaadn (Katahdin), the highest point in the state. More so than Petrarch's day-trip or Fabre's overnight adventure, in the mid-nineteenth century an ascent of Mount Ktaadn was an extremely hazardous venture: the region was remote and for the most part uninhabited, uncharted, unexplored—"like a desolate island, and No-Mans Land"[40]—and the journey was physically arduous, upriver and with much portage through trailless forests. The description of the mountain is not unlike that of the Ventoux: "The mountain seemed a vast aggregation of loose rocks, as if some time it had rained rocks, and they lay as they fell on the mountain sides, nowhere fairly at rest, but leaning on each other, all rocking-stones, with cavities between, but scarcely any soil or smoother shelf."[41] Thoreau describes the experience in terms inhuman, extrahuman, mythic, divine: "It reminded me of the creations of the old epic and dramatic poets, of Atlas, Vulcan, the Cyclops, and Prometheus."[42] Time present seemed to depend on epochs past. But rather than being an ode to the beauties and wonders of creation, Mount Ktaadn is something very different, since here, "there is no shrine, no altar," and "the tops of mountains are among the unfinished parts of the globe, whither it is a slight insult to the gods to climb and pry into their secrets, and try their effects on our humanity."[43] These are rare sites of chaos and formlessness, incomprehensible and uncanny. Literature becomes their shrine.

Thoreau does well to cite the ancients, but he neglects the actual source of this vision of the mountain as a vast ruin, Lucretius's *De*

Rerum Natura, in which mountains are characterized as the waste places of the world.[44] This notion reached its apogee in a now nearly forgotten work that was immensely influential on the romantic theory of the sublime, Thomas Burnet's *The Sacred Theory of the Earth* (1684), in which the author attempts to reconcile biblic interpretation with scientific discovery:

> These Mountains are plac'd in no Order one with another, that can either respect Use or Beauty; and if you consider them singly, they do not consist of any Proportion of Parts that is referable to any Design, or that hath the least Footsteps of Art or Counsel. There is nothing in Nature more shapeless and ill-figur'd than an old Rock or Mountain, and all that Variety that is among them, is but the many various Modes of Irregularity; so as you can not make a better Character of them, in short, than to say they are of all Forms and Figures except regular. . . . And lastly, if you look upon an Heap of them together, or a mountainous Country, they are the greatest Examples of Confusion that we know in Nature; no Tempest or Earthquake puts Things into more Disorder.[45]

While Burnet bemoaned the postdiluvian imperfections of the globe, epitomized by the horrendous, unformed excrescences of the mountains as a sign of primal human sin, Thoreau would experience there the purity of the last parts of the globe unspoiled by humans.

After the descent, and already engaged on the return journey, Thoreau meditated upon the mountain he had just climbed, but hardly conquered: "This was the Earth of which we have heard, made out of Chaos and Old Night. Here was no man's garden, but the unhandseled globe [. . . .] Man was not to be associated with it."[46] Here, many others would have evoked the sublime. But as much as Thoreau's heritage was that of romanticism, his theistic transcendentalist appreciation of nature had no need of the sublime to evoke the deepest emotions. Rather, Thoreau's seemingly antithetical passion for precise observation of the natural world allusively linked to a heterogeneous host of mythologies would give rise to a particular richness in his writings. Indeed, the sublime—with its blinding presence and its stultifying terror—is the antithesis of mythic thought, which functions precisely through subtle differentiations, significant correspondences, and intricate narratives. It is also the antithesis of the scientific spirit, where categorization is a function of comparison, and identification a function of differentiation; where blindness is a physiological, and not a mystical, state; and where even the void itself must be measured, whether in barometric pressure or astronomic measure. But as Fabre and Thoreau reveal through their writings, there is poetry on both sides of the equation.

Fabre presents the Ventoux in terms of a striking oppositon: the panoptical splendor of the view from the peak versus the total blindness caused by the storm. A second opposition will enrich the first. The mountain is early on in the text geologically described as a "heap of shattered stones," where "the cascades of the Ventoux are streamings of rubble; the rumbling of tumbling rocks replaces the murmur of the waters."[47] It is an empty rocky mass, pure scree. Yet conversely, in botanical terms, the Ventoux is all revealing, a veritable panopticon of plant life. For as one ascends from the base to the summit, one passes through all the botanic levels—from submediterranean through subalpine—representing the entire range of plant life that one would discover on a long northward voyage following a single meridian from the Mediterranean coast through the arctic regions. So Petrarch did go north after all, by climbing the Ventoux! His ultimate rejection of altitude was therefore congruous with his hatred of the north.

But there is a final opposition elucidated by Fabre, perhaps the most stunning of all. During the month of July, the mountain's spring, the peak of the Ventoux—that pile of stone seemingly above the vegetation line; that often snow-covered, always windswept, eminently uninhabitable peak; that epitome of emptiness and disappearance—is transformed into a veritable flower bed. At that moment, the rocky peak is totally covered with flowers: *Androsace villosa,* whose white blossoms seem to glance out at the botanist with tender rose eyes; *Viola cenisia,* whose large blue corollas are in striking contrast with the harsh whiteness of the rocks; *Valerianeae saliunca,* an odorific oxymoron, since the gentle perfume of its flowers is the antithesis of the fecal odor of its roots; *Globularia cordifolia,* forming a compact green carpet strewn with blue capitula; *Myosotis alpestris,* of an azure rivalling that of the heavens; *Iberis Candolleana,* tiny white flowers that plunge, serpentine, amidst the rocks; *Saxifraga oppositifolia* and *Saxifraga muscoides,* small, dark cushions, the former constellated with rose, and the latter with yellowish white, corollas.

It is as if the Ventoux—that empty, violent, horrifying void—were magically transformed, through an ascent inspired by scientific observation, through an all-too-rational *coincidentia oppositorum*, into the plenitude of a universal garden. The passage of the seasons, the ascent of the mountain, leads from absence to presence. Such is truly the work of *metaphor*, in the literal sense of the term—transfer, replacement, representation—a mental operation from which scientific description is hardly exempt. The Provençal harshness of the Ventoux disappears; it is as if the Ventoux were magically metamorphosed into the lush botanical extravagence of an alpine meadow. The sublime is transmuted into the picturesque.

Afterwards, the ascent continues; Febre mounts from the earthly element to the celestial spheres, moving towards a certain transcendence, as he evokes the hardly scientific domain of the ancient gods. For science too has its poetry, often apparent as the vestigial traces of myth and religion condense into the very names its gives its creatures, a Latinate poetry of quasi-Adamic nomination. He concludes with an apparition, simultaneously poetic and entomological, reminding us that at the highest altitudes of the Ventoux, when the sun is present in its late spring force, there appears the flowery shimmering of a superb butterfly that usually haunts the Alpine solitudes of eternal snow, a butterfly whose white wings are beautifully stained with four carmine spots encircled with black, a creature that detaches itself from the flowery earth to float towards the glimmering heavens: the *Parnassius Apollo*.

III

Metaphor

> Wouldn't the geographic sentiment be the confused certainty that every reverie bears its own earth?
>
> —Michel Chaillou, *Le sentiment geographique*

It is curious that none of the critics, whether benevolent or malevolent, of my Unnatural Horizons: Paradox and Contradiction in Landscape Architecture, *noted that each chapter of this book ends with the disappearance of the landscape: the Italian Renaissance garden disappears within the textual labyrinth of a web of icons and symbols, emblems and myths; the Baroque garden is sublimated by pure spiritualization and dematerialization, absorbed into the vortices of the celestial azure; the eighteenth-century libertine garden is assimilated into an erotic utopia, reduced to an instrumental aid to seduction; Thoreau's notion of untouched nature is belied by the historical conditions in which it arises, a landscape already scarred, mythically and really, by those locomotives that traversed the country, such that the virgin forest is truly "no man's garden"; and the modernist garden, in its heterotopic splendor, is evidence of that oxymoron of a hyperbolically denatured nature, dominated by the demon of Time, revealing the innate contradictions of landscape as representation. It is also curious that none of the book's critics, whether benevolent or malevolent, realized that a book on gardens and landscape could well inspire, along with gardening and landscaping, reverie and writing. While the landscape might vanish behind its metaphors, it always exists through its images and allegories, its deliria and dreams. What I learned from all this is that "nowhere" can truly constitute a locale.*

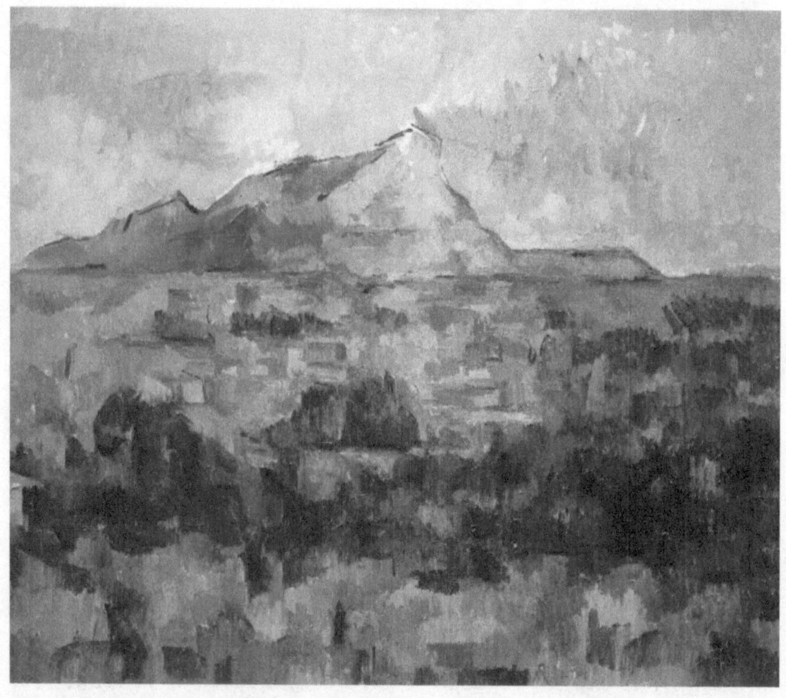

FIGURE 11. Paul Cezanne, *Mount Sainte-Victoire*, 1906.
Private collection, Zurich, Switzlerland.
Photo credit: Erich Lessing/Art Resource, NY.

"Le Mont Ventoux, miroir des aigles, était en vue." (Mont Ventoux, mirror of the eagles, was in sight.)[1] This declaration, from René Char's poem "Le Thor," is perhaps the most beautiful expression of Mont Ventoux. But what does this metaphor mean? Does the mountain somehow reveal the eagles to themselves? But this would be to denature the mountain. Are the eagles' shadows upon the peak their reflections? But this would be a weak metaphor, taking the less-articulated shadow for the more-defined reflection. Is it a matter of resemblance between the white heads of the eagles and the Ventoux's stunning white peak?[2] But this would be to offer a very common visual denominator as the most striking image? Might the eagles harken back to those in Mistral's *Calendau?* "Lis aiglo en gingoulant s'enauron dins lis èr" (The shrieking eagles rise in the air.)[3] Char would certainly have had little motivation for alluding to the outmoded, overtraditional, musty poetic style and narrow regionalism of the Felibres. Might the eagle be a symbol of transcendence? Char was not one to use readymade metaphors. The context hardly helps, as this mirror image is seen on the horizon of a herb-lined path near Le Thor—the town where Heidegger would, years later, give his famous seminar while in France—where, "the chimera of a lost age smiled at our young tears,"[4] an observation that, rather than informing the metaphor, only complicates it. In a sense, the emptiest context creates the richest symbols, since the undecidability of meaning multiplies the potential complexity of semantic content. Thus the eagle appears here in the full glory of its symbolism: ascensional, flying above the clouds, it is a celestial sign of divine transcendence; sovereign, fixing the sun, it invokes the illumination of supersensible knowledge; vast wings outstretched, its form evokes both the holy cross and the lightning flash; soaring, diving, disappearing beyond the horizon, it bears initiatory, tutelary, mantic powers; in the Bible, four of the angels described in Ezekiel's vision bear both "the face of an eagle" and "the appearance of a flash of lightening" (*Ezekiel,* 1:10), yet the symbolic inversion of this figure also makes of it a sign of the Antichrist. However, none of these readings is warranted by the context. In Char's line, the stark syntax and minimal context create a polyvalent symbol in an open field of virtualities. The mirror, here identified with the Ventoux itself, is an archetypal figure of the chiasm (chiasmus), formed by the exact inversion of syntactic elements (AB/BA) so as to establish a reflective, reflexive structure. This makes of it an exemplary figure of mimesis. Consequently it is, as Jean-François Lyotard explains, "the figure constitutive of the sensible, the figure constitutive of figures."[5] It is also transformative, a "magic" mirror, reflecting death in life, transcendence in immanence, the supersensible in the sensible. However, for such reversibility between object and image, reality and appearance, to exist within the chiasm, the mirror must disappear: only the broken mirror has its own existence. In "Le Thor," the mirror is conflated with the mountain, which reflects nothing, thus voiding the mirror of its essence, creating a false chiasm and a complex metaphor. As for the Ventoux itself, its semantic content is already so meager, so underdetermined, as to reinforce the ambiguity. What at first appears to be a simple metaphor, graspable in its unity, is in fact equivocal, undeterminable, unstable. This is typical of Char's rhetoric, where determinations often tend towards the emblematic, and meanings towards the semi-universal; this is a privileged type of rhetorical usage in twentieth-century poetry: latent metaphoricity animated by complex ambiguity.[6] The power of Char's "mirror" resides precisely in its inexactitude, in the fact that it barely holds together, causing a linguistic instability most appropriate to expess *a mountain that has always resisted revelation through metaphor*. In fact, Char's metaphor both complicates the privileged topos of Petrarch's poetry—the azimuth between mountain and sky, earth and heaven, ground and transcendence—and enriches Petrarch's equivocation between sacred and profane experiences of mountain peaks. This is an anxious space, uncertain, fluctuating in signification: the space of poetry, of language itself.

René Char lived practically his entire life in the presence of Mont Ventoux, but there are not even a dozen references to this mountain in his work.[7] In a rare autobiographical statement of substance, Char reveals a moment of family history not without impact on his poetics, one which might well be taken as part of the unconscious of his work. His grandfather was, at the age of ten, a shepherd on the slopes of the Ventoux, when one night a wolf ate one of his lambs. The terrified child hid all night in a cave, with the wolves prowling outside. Understandably, he subsequently found work elsewhere.[8] Thus Char's only tale of human events on Mont Ventoux is one of violence and flight from the mountain. Like Petrarch, Char was warned away from the Ventoux by a shepherd. Also like Petrarch, Char chose the Sorgue as his preferred landscape, the place of his home, the name of his myth, the source of his creativity. Writing of the inspiration behind *Feuillets d'Hypnos* and *Partage formel*—the poetry and prose Char wrote while an officer in the French resistance fighting in the Alps—Gabriel Bounoure notes that, "We take the maquis of the Alps as one of the high places of French poetry."[9] One might well wonder whether the same might be said of Mont Ventoux, the mountain on the horizon of most of Char's other verse. Bounoure well expresses the effects of mountains on the poetic temperament:

> At this altitude the poetic word becomes hard, tightens upon itself, without ornament, without lyrical softness, without oratorical padding [. . . .] It is this climate full of nothingness and of energy that, for the "point set with diamonds" of poetic consciousness, gives back to the inflections of the Sorgue all their value of seduction and enfolding. This presence "through oneself" is necessary so that the partisan can set out towards the summits, towards the "high points," as soldiars say. The only means of writings poems from the base. The eagle's nest, a privileged place from which to see and love the carnal folds, the curve of riverbanks, the plain and its harvests.[10]

But, as for Petrarch, these inhuman, transcendent summits need be forgotten in order to write—otherwise one risks the incommunicable vocables of the mystics, or the empty generalizations of the philosophers. Bounoure then quotes Char on the relation between ascent and descent: "While we are apt to climb towards an initatory summit with the aid of some natural ladder, we leave below the lower echelons; but when we redescend, we force all the echelons of the summit to slide down with us."[11] The experience from the summit is an abstraction from materiality that permits transcendence; the perspective from the base is of a human plenitude that bears traces, however unconscious, of that transcendence. Char chose the Sorgue, not the Ventoux.

> Rivière trop tôt partie, d'une traite, sans compagnon,
> Donne aux enfants de mon pays le visage de ta passion.[12]
>
> [River too soon departed, straight off, without companion,
> Give to the children of my land the face of your passion.]

In an appropriately entitled volume, *La fontaine narrative* [The Narrative Fountain, 1947], he explains in a prose poem, "Les premiers instants" [The First Instants]: "We see the rising water flow before us. It effaces the mountain in a single stroke, chasing itself from its maternal sides."[13] Is the mountain in question among the Alpine ones, still all too recent in his scarred memory, or is it the Ventoux, once again back in his sight? Paul Veyne, in his study *René Char en ses poèmes* [René Char in His Poetry], makes an astonishing transposition in this regard, writing of the poem "La Sorgue": "The veritable Sorgue has its source at Fontaine-de-Vaucluse and surrounds L'Isle [L'Isle-sur-Sorgue] on three sides. The Sorgue of the poem is so little a river that is would be permissible, without changing its meaning, to replace it with a mountain, by Mont Ventoux, on the northern horizon, that isolated summit at the extremity of the Alpine foreland, whose slopes are covered with masses of rocky debris. . . ."[14] This is an extraordinary idea, insofar as in metaphor and allegory it is the Ventoux that has always disappeared. For the first time, the trajectory of the metaphor is reversed: the Sorgue permits its true poetic source, the Ventoux, to exist, and the Alps give materiality to their strange Provençal counterpart, Mont Ventoux. In order to elucidate the hidden truth behind Char's poetry, Veyne—who has long lived at the foot of Mont Ventoux—needed to reveal its transcendental source, in apparent conflict with Char's mythos. Veyne suggests that like the Montagne Sainte-Victoire for Cézanne, Mont Ventoux marked Char's imagination as the unity behind the multiplicity of appearances. In a profound intuition, Veyne maintains that "The Ventoux will remain the symbol of the ideal, of the unity of all values, of Poetry."[15] How is it possible that this mountain, so recalcitrant to representation, could play such a fundamental role?

Summits offer the broadest horizons, the greatest visibility, the widest openness: such are the physical manifestations of transcendence, eminently accessible to poetry. The eagle, however uncommonly mirrored by the mountain, always disappears beyond the horizon or into the heights. It disappears into the open, as does the Ventoux. There are some places whose genius it is to hide. There are some places deserted by the gods, as Mistral has shown might be the curse of the Ventoux. And there are some epochs when the gods themselves desert the earth. One never knows the exact date when a god is forgotten: oblivion exists in stages. Char, following in the modernist tradition of Hölderlin, Nietzsche and Heidegger, believes that the gods have withdrawn from the earth: "The gods neither decline nor die, but, with an imperious and cyclical movement, like the ocean, withdraw."[16] These are "intermittent gods,"[17] gods that exist only through metaphor,[18] such that Char can claim, in open paradox: "I submit to my gods who do not exist."[19] Unlike mountains that manifest themselves in the formalism and plenitude of images (such as Cézanne's Sainte-Victoire), Char's Ventoux, like the gods, needs to hide. Transcendence must be occluded for modernist poetry to exist. This is perhaps best stated by Maurice Blanchot writing on the birth of philosophy in Char's poetry, stressing the originary violence that marks the genesis of a poem. This obtains in a double movement, simultaneously the exultation of opening forth and the withdrawal into the depths of dissimulation: ". . . the work is an intimateness struggling with irreconcilable and inseperable moments, a communication torn between the measure of the work that becomes power and what is beyond measure in the work, that which desires impossibility—between the form through which it is grasped and the limitlessness where it is refused, between the work as beginning and the origin from which no work is ever derived—where an eternal idleness *[désoeuvrement]* reigns."[20] Might the Ventoux not be the site of, the expression of, such originary violence? Between form and the unlimited, between the concrete and the ideal, lies an opposition at the core of language itself. Isn't this opposition between materiality and transcendence precisely the antinomy that underlies all of Western philosophy? The Ventoux—stupendous and evanescent, awe-inspiring and bleak—might serve as the emblem of all symbols that unite materiality and transcendence. The Ventoux might even be the very allegory of allegory. This is precisely the illumination that both Petrarch and Char experienced on its peak: that the impression of limitlessness, of transcendence, of the infinite, of the sublime, is always bound to a place, and that *the gods need to be dismissed so that the poet may write.*

A curious transposition occurs in Pierre Michon's book, *Trois auteurs* [Three Authors], one section of which, "La danseuse," is partially devoted to Petrarch. He begins by referring to Charles-Albert Cingria's book *Pétrarque:* "Cingria used images that changed from one text to the other and were chosen in function of their immediate context:

Mont Ventoux to accompany the promenades of Petrarch. . . ."[21] Yet when we finally come to the passage that speaks of Petrarch, fully expecting Michon to continue writing about the famed experience of the Ventoux, we read: "On 19 April 1353, at the third [ecclesiastic] hour of the day, that is, near nine in the morning, Petrarch walked in the countryside, on the road that leads from Aix to Saint-Maximin [. . . .] One is in the universe, the universe is vast, and as one strides across it, it is sensible: one desires this sense of the world, such is the intangible object of deambulation, of poetics, and of theology. On your left, that elevated mass of almond trees, of bald rocks and birds, is not just any chaos, it is the Montagne Sainte-Victoire in spring."[22] The Montagne Sainte-Victoire, not Mont Ventoux! Michon alludes to the road that Cézanne followed so many times, so as to paint order into that "chaos." Scree, birds, chaos: this could be Mont Ventoux, or Mount Ktaadn, or so many others. At first reading, the shift from the expectation of Mont Ventoux to the apparition of the Montagne Sainte-Victoire seems rather curious, a mere dramatic effect that just happens to coincide with the Ventoux's long history of disappearances. This would seem to be a prime example of what Merleau-Ponty termed "the occult trading of the metaphor—where what counts is no longer the manifest meaning of each word and of each image, but the lateral relations, the kinships that are implicated in their transfers and exchanges."[23] Not only all landscape poetry, not only all etymology of place names, but all thought follows these rules of indirectness and reversibility, of dispossession and ephemerality. Indeed, perhaps this conflation of mountains is not so strange after all.

Etymology often reveals destiny. Charles Rostaing, in his *Essai sur la toponymie en Provence,* explains: "La racine *VIN*—'mountain' is well known: Trombetti cites Mount *Vindius* in Iberia where today we find Vignemale. In Provence two names of mountains refer to this root: Mont Ventoux *(Vinturi)* and the Montagne Sainte-Victoire, a late transcription of Ventúri. Both derive from a stem *VIN-T-,* like Vindius. We find this stem in certain place names in Provence. . . ."[24] More specifically, consider the following etymological analysis of the Ventoux, offered by Camille Jullian:

> The Sainte-Victoire, that of Aix, derives, I believe, from a celtic or ligurian word such as *Ventur, Venturius,* or something similar. The primitive name of the mountain was never *Victoria* [. . . .] When one finds a mountain under its true local and Provençal form [. . .] it is called

> *Ventùri* or *Sancto Ventùri,* and never otherwise [. . . .] I thus consider the name *Ventùri,* from the Latin *Ventur* or *Venturius,* as the true and primitive name of the Montagne Sainte-Victoire [. . . .] *Ventùri* and *Ventur* are one and the same. And in the past the distance between these two words diminishes even more. On maps the Ventoux was called *Venturius* and, during the Roman era, *Vintur* [. . . .] Sainte-Victoire and Mont Ventoux [. . .] both bore the same celtic or ligurian name at their origin, a most appropriate name for those summits from which the clouds and the wind seem to arise.[25]

Mont Ventoux and the Montagne Sainte-Victoire are one and the same! Furthermore, these two bald mountains which so resemble each other, and which both dominate their respective landscapes, are not only both believed to be connected by underground currents—that archteypal metaphor of unconscious intuition and creativity—to Fountaine-de-Vaucluse, but it is also believed that an entrance to hell is to be found within caves in each of these mountains.[26] In every place there is an absent place, and every place is always the symbol of another. North and south, Celtic and Ligurian, resonate with each others' myths. Not only are Mont Ventoux (near the northern limit of Provence) and the Montagne Sainte-Victoire (near its southern limit) one and the same, but *all the mountains of Provence are named Ventoux!* This is metaphor in the literal and prolific sense of the word: *metapherein,* transfer, change. The Sainte-Victoire loses its original name and gains a false identity; the Ventoux keeps its name but hides its true identity, driving away all those who wish to sing its praise, always seeking invisibility, ever eschewing representation. *The Ventoux is not only itself: it is also a generality, a tautology, the very mountain of mountains.*

Consider another, more theologically oriented etymological suggestion. As is popularly believed, and as meteorology well attests, Mont Ventoux is named after the northerly wind. We learn this from Marjorie Leach's *Guide to the Gods:* "Vintios, Vintius. A Celtic god of the wind identified with Pollux. Gaul."[27] *The mountain and the wind are, paradoxically, one and the same.* It is as if the mistral blowing over the mountain is Vinturius caressing himself. Michel Clerc expands on this etymology:

> The true name of Mont Ventoux, still seen on eighteenth century maps, is not Ventoux, but *Ventour.* And this name undoubtedly

> derives from the name of the divinity Venturius, to whom are dedicated two Roman inscriptions found in Mirabel, near Vaison, and at Buoux, in the north of the Luberon. It is not impossible that this divinity was not only that of Mont Ventoux, but the general divinity of mountains in the entire Provençal region, a divinity of Celtic, or rather Ligurian, origin. The name derives, without a doubt, from a root analogous to the Latin *ventus*. At Mont Ventoux this ancient name was conserved; at Sainte-Victoire it was transformed under a double influence, that of the continual work of erudition, and that of the local clergy, whose acts were no less efficient.[28]

The history and etymological shift of the Sainte-Victoire are telling. Until the seventeenth century, the Montagne Sainte-Victoire was called Mont Venture, or to give it a Christian form, Mont Sainte-Venture. On its summit was a small chapel dedicated to its namesake. In the 1650s a rich bourgeois from Aix made a vow to restore the chapel if he recovered from a disease. When he did recover, he saw to the restoration and bestowed upon the restored chapel the name of Notre-Dame de Sainte-Victoire, since the Virgin was sometimes referred to in terms of "Victoire" after 1629, when Louis XIII began construction of Notre-Dame-des-Victoires in praise of Mary's help in his triumph over the Protestants. A common linguistic slippage took place in the seventeenth century, when the mountain took on the name of the chapel, Sainte-Victoire. In the nineteenth century, another pseudo-historic layer was added, following the popular belief that the victory in question was that of Marius over the Teutonic invaders in the year 102 B.C. The mountain, originally dedicated to the pagan god of the wind, lost its identity—first usurped by the Christian god, then through commemoration of a proto-Provençal victory, and finally by being definitively recuperated by local popular Christian traditions. Transformed by the infinite powers of the Christian god, the Montagne Sainte-Victoire would be a premature tumulus for the god Vintius, as so many other mountains were for so many gods before him.

One anecdote relating to this confusion is particularly charming and revealing. Already by the seventeenth century, the inhabitants of the town of Pertuis founded a pilgrimage group called the Venturiers, which continued to exist through the Second Empire. Their major ritual consisted of climbing to the summit of the Sainte-Victoire each Midsummer night to celebrate the feast of Saint John's Eve. Following a tradition that exists throughout Europe, they would light a bonfire on the summit; here, in addition, another fire was lit in the village below, an earthly blaze in response to the celestial one. They would then crown themselves with flowers and dance a farandole. As André Bouyala d'Arnauld notes, "Through their name, 'Venturiers,' they evoked the old indigenous appellation of Mont Venture. In their good faith they believed they were celebrating, on the mountain's summit, the victory of Marius. But in fact, what they were celebrating up there, without knowing it, was the ancient festival of the sun, the summer solstice, in direct union with local folklore."[29] Those fires, lit to celebrate the bounty of the Christian god, also glorified, whether surreptitiously or unconsciously, the pagan gods in a ritual of purification and fertility. To light a huge bonfire on top of a mountain during the first days of summer is to intensify the heat and sublime or sublimate the earth, so as to create the conjunction of earth and sky through flame and smoke. For the smoke from sacrifice and oblation is a mediation between human and divine, low and high, profane and sacred. Paradoxically, this smoke simultaneously creates a link between humanity and divinity *and* assures the absolute separation between the two. It is said: "Erect an altar, and a god shall come." But indeed, occasionally, one god hides behind the rituals of another.

Having grown up in a German peasant milieu essentially deprived of images, Peter Handke came to wonder about the relation between endlessly repeated ornamentation and his striving for the infinite: "And is it not a perfectly colorless and formless void that can most miraculously come to life?"[30] As soon as he began to appreciate paintings, he immediately preferred landscapes, particularly those, "suggesting the depopulated, silently beautiful, menacing phantasms of half-sleep"—works by de Chirico, Ernst, Magritte, Hopper.[31] In accord with this iconography of solitude and mystery, Handke also heeded the word of "the philosopher" (Heidegger?), a philosophy fraught with the most extreme moral implications in the latter part of the twentieth century: "To uproot others, he said, was the worst of crimes; to uproot oneself, the greatest of achievements."[32] Handke would subsequently undertake a voyage of self-deracination, one specifically linked to the desire to write. The outcome would be the "lesson" he learned from the Montagne Sainte-Victoire. Writing expressly in contrast to the Ventoux (which he only mentions in passing, as being visible from the slopes of the Sainte-Victoire): "Mont *[sic]* Sainte-Victoire is not the highest mountain in Provence, but it is said to be the steepest."[33] Why the choice of the Sainte-Victoire over the Ventoux—which is indeed the culminating point of Provence—in a quest for "the perfect void"? We find the answer is his belief in the transformative nature of art: "Isn't the spot where a great artist worked the center of the world—rather than places like Delphi?"[34] Handke preferred graven images to prophetic sayings. He chose the Sainte-Victoire because it was already represented; he chose that mountain because of the proof that it was eminently representable; he chose it because of Cézanne's immense work in creating the plenitude that we now experience in the face of this bald mountain. Perhaps he chose it precisely so as not to have to face the void.

Handke sought a unity of object, painting, writing, gesture; the overdetermined, not the empty, signifier; plenitude, not emptiness. This sort of geographic inspiration had recently received brilliant expression in Michel Chaillou's book, *Le sentiment géographique,* a meditation, indeed a reverie, on Honoré d'Urfé's seventeenth-century novel *L'Astrée.* It is precisely the unity of landscape, image, writing, promenade, and reverie that, for Chaillou, is the essence of literature:

> . . . you shall then know from within yourself, without any longer needing to measure your steps against ours, how to recognize those monuments in this confused region, enigmatic because partially dreamt, the impression of the already-touched progressively replacing that of the already-read, as words become weighed down with turf, as the sentence becomes a path, its meaning a direction in the grass anciently crushed under a couched person where the heteroclite nature of apparitions ("*Quite often one figure surges forth from another,*" Marie de Manacéïne, *Le Sommeil tiers de notre vie,* p. 253) is explained by the mingling of a book and a country, from that sleeplessness and that sleep propitious to mixed creatures: Satyrs with goats' feet, Faunes and Sylvans (a Latin inscription celebrating this latter rustic divinity was, in fact, discovered at Feurs), hypnagogic creatures born from the brain of the Great Pan awakening through the pastoral of your closing eyes, of your tentative gestures aided by a shepherd's crook, of your lips playing an air more inspired than expired, inspired by Honoré d'Urfé. . . .[35]

What is discovered at the heights of mountaintops is also found in the depths of sleep: an isolation that does not offer tranquility in solitude, but rather a purity, a crystallization of self awash in anguish, an *angst* that facets words according to an errant, supramundane imagination. The "meanders" of the imagination take on new meaning. In other words, as the landscape artist Robert Smithson said so succinctly: "Words and rocks contain a language that follows a syntax of splits and ruptures. Look at any *word* long enough and you will see it open up into a series of faults, into a terrain of particles each containing its own void."[36] This opening of the word is determined by the function of writing and the structure of rhetoric. Handke would seek his own conflation of rock and word, path and sentence.

What Handke admired in Cézanne was such a unity of image, thought, and gesture; this was Handke's secret literary ideal, precisely what he sought on the slopes of the Sainte-Victoire. "As I studied the maps and descriptions of the mountain, my thoughts began, involuntarily and inexplicably, to revolve around one and the same point: a fault between two strata of different kinds of rock."[37] While this fracture was invisible to the naked eye, it appeared time and again in Cézanne's paintings and drawings, a "shadow line" akin, one might add, to that "thin, pale line" of Mallarmé's poetry. Handke returned to Provence in order to accommodate the visible with the invisible, and climbed the Montagne Sainte-Victoire for the same reason that Petrarch climbed Mont Ventoux: to reconcile immanence and transcendence. There Handke discovered the icon that made this possible, a mere rift, a crack, a fissure, a fault: "Gradually the gap in the distant crest transferred itself to me and became a pivot."[38] What began as the mortal fear of being crushed between two sediments of rock ended with a profound feeling of "openness, of a single all-enveloping breath."[39] Like the Christians of Pertuis in the guise of Venturiers and like Cézanne in his daily confrontations with the familiar mountain, Handke made the Sainte-Victoire his own. If he didn't quite inhabit it, he at least permitted it to dwell within himself. He might well have said, following those words of Cézanne worthy of the best of Petrarch's quasi-divine personifications, and in the lineage of Mallarmé's relation to the totality of the Spiritual Universe: "The landscape thinks itself in me, and I am its consciousness." But in any case, it was precisely the landscape that permitted Handke to write: not by providing a *tabula rasa,* but rather by establishing that openness, that rift, that imperfection, that void which is the overture of word and thought. The fault in the rock led to the truth in the word.

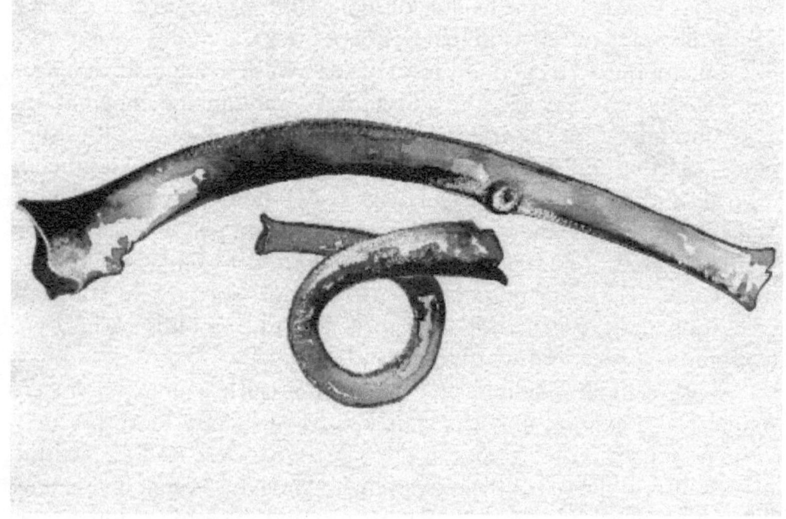

FIGURE 12. Terra-cotta trumpets found on the peak of Mont Ventoux.

The opening paragraph of Char's "Les dentelles de Montmirail"—referring to the bizarre mountainous rock formations immediately to the west of Mont Ventoux—reads: "*At the summit of the mount, amongst the pebbles, terra-cotta trumpets of the men of the ancient white frosts chirped like little eagles.*"[40] Amongst the many objects sold to the British museum in 1901 by the French researcher and collector L. Morel are two terra-cotta trumpets discovered during an excavation on the peak of Mont Ventoux. These horns, similar to many others found in the region, are a type of primitive megaphone of Celtic origin, anciently used to herald the spring. How were they ritually used? Perhaps they were blown to drive away the mistral, a small, short, pathetic human breath disproportionately pitted against that eternal, divine, powerful, maddening wind. Or perhaps they were sounded in harmony with the mistral, as an act of sympathetic magic, in order to divert some of the god's powers for human purposes. In either case, at the end of the rite they were violently shattered against the rocky peak of the Ventoux. The trumpet that breathed the human wind was smashed against the mountain that bore the wind's very name. Only one of these trumpets was ever found intact. What could this mean? Did one year bring a disaster that precluded the ritual, with the trumpet transfixed in its perfect form, like those tragically preserved objects eternally covered with lava and ash at Pompeii and Herculaneum? Does its wholeness imply a spring that never came? Or perhaps at some point did men just stop bothering to announce the spring, a moment that quietly announced the forgetting of yet another god?

As god of the wind, Vinturius cannot be precisely localized: he is one of the rare gods whose essence is detachment from place. He is a god without an altar, without source or season, without a face. Paradoxically, the *genius loci* of Mont Ventoux is Vinturius, a god who does not inhabit the mountain, a god omnipresent in Provence, a god whose very essence is uprootedness, the detachment from place, from all places—a god who is everywhere and nowhere. The destiny of that other "Ventoux," the Sainte-Victoire, was to be the site of the struggle between two unlocalizable pneumatic gods, between two gods who manifest themselves as air, wind, breath, spirit: the now forgotten Vinturius, and the Christian god, whose far greater domain was ecumenical and seemingly universal. Thus the battle was immeasurably unequal: the perceptible *pneuma* of Vinturius was pure wind, and thus unarticulated, while the immaterial *pneuma* of the Christian god was the Word, the thundering word—that which separated the heavens from the earth and organized the originary chaos from which our world arose—an articulated wind that demanded sublimation and worship, an articulated wind that we, speaking creatures, could easily identify with, could easily reproduce, could easily imitate. Vinturius, eloquent yet inarticulate, long forgotten because ineffable, lost the battle at the Montagne Sainte-Victoire centuries ago. But by some quirk of history—some "dead-end" in the historical dialectic, as Merleau-Ponty would say—Vinturius never quite lost its aerian hold on Mont Ventoux, that rare site which has resisted representation over the centuries. Perhaps he survived because as wind he was invisible, intermittent, inexorable, and it was at the Ventoux, equally unrepresentable, that he blew the strongest, in divine empathy with the mountain. *Ventoux, mirror of Vinturius*. Perhaps he survived because as wind he was almost silent, thus concealed: not thunder, but breath. Perhaps he survived because, as Char always believed, certain gods exist only through metaphor, and are thus always elsewhere.[41]

René Char was fascinated by lightening. Paul Veyne, in a poetic act of friendship, used to call him whenever lightning struck Mont Ventoux, so as to let him know that the storm would soon be over Char's house.[42] Lightning, enlightenment, illumination, intuition, inspiration: perhaps, surmises Veyne, Char so loved Giorgione's painting *The Tempest* for its single, mysterious lightning flash.[43] Might Char have been inspired by Horace's wondrous observation?: "The tops of pines affront the great wind; the high towers collapse with a roar; and lightning strikes the summits of mountains."

In December 1987, as Veyne was at work on his book about Char's poetry, they met as they had done so many times before, in friendship and collaboration. Char began the conversation by noting that for several weeks the Ventoux had been covered, totally hidden from sight, and then inquired about the stand of oaks behind Veyne's house that, complained Char, both hid the Ventoux from Veyne and dissimulated Veyne from the Ventoux. Then, unexpectedly and most disturbingly, in a voice other than his own, Char ripped into a long tirade against Veyne and his book. Veyne could hardly fathom his words. This was the last time the two would meet. Two months later Char was dead.[44] He is buried near the Sorgue, source of his inspiration. In homage, we should remember the belief that the source of the Sorgue is to be found in the depths of Mont Ventoux.

IV

Breath

. . . to airy nothing /A local habitation and a name.
—William Shakespeare,
A Midsummer Night's Dream

Several years ago, I was intrigued by the extraordinary reading of the irregular wave patterns on sixth-century B.C. *Ionico-Massalian pottery offered by Gustaf Sobin in* Luminous Debris: *these waves represent an originary rhythm, before rationalizing Greek thought would regulate motion by transmuting it into cadence, meter, good form. The rhythm of these waves—before* Logos *succumbed to the rule of* Eidos*—revealed "the fluid architecture of each given instance," a rhythm characterized as, "iridescent chaos, as Cézanne once put it: a place from which the virginity of the world might, once again, be experienced."*[1] *I knew not why at the time, but these meditations spoke to something that had been profoundly troubling me about the Ventoux project, so I contacted the author. He generously entered into correspondence, and sent, as an offering, a copy of his book of poetry,* The Earth as Air, *whose title is an unusually suggestive oxymoron, bearing all the contradictions of the fact that the god Vinturius inhabits both wind and mountain. It was inscribed to me with the following words:* "Per fumum, *through smoke."*

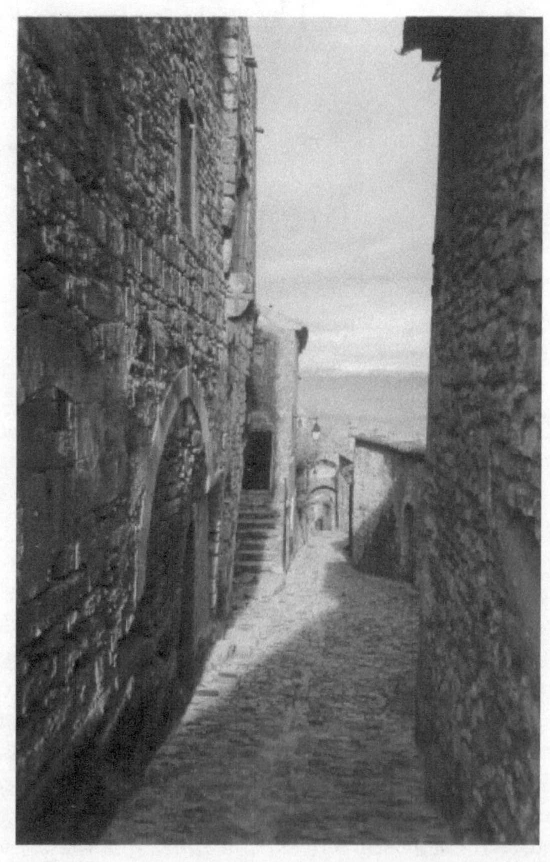

FIGURE 13. Mont Ventoux seen from Lacoste.

"It seems that it is the sky that has the last word. But it is pronounced in a voice so low that no one ever hears it."[2] So writes Char in "Les Dentelles de Montmirail," just after mention of the broken terra-cotta trumpets found on the summit of Mont Ventoux. This voice is the whisper of the wind.

There are poets of the wind, poets who celebrate the very breath of the word. Gaston Bachelard, in *L'air et les songes* [Air and Dreams], suggests that "to all immanence is joined a transcendence." It is the role of the aerian imagination to articulate this metaphysical relationship at the heart of poetry.

> It is the very law of poetic expression to surpass thought. Without a doubt, this transcendence often appears as rough, false, broken. Sometimes it also succeeds too quickly, it is illusory, evaporated, dispersive. For the reflective being, it is a mirage. But this mirage fascinates. It entails a special dynamic, which is already an undeniable psychological reality. One could therefore class poets according to their response to the question: "Tell me which is your infinity, and I shall know the meaning of your universe. Is it the infinity of the sea or the sky, is it the infinity of the depths of the earth or of the pyre?"[3]

According to what Bachelard terms the "dynamics of dematerialization," the pure aerian imagination is allied to infinity, to total openness, to emptiness; and it unfolds its elemental corollary in the open sky, the azure of the heavens, the black of the moonless night.[4] This is a solitary, imageless, iconoclastic imagination, a form of poetic meditation that replaces the Cartesian "method of doubt" with a "method of erasure."[5] Air is the element of lightness, of the ephemeral, inspiring dreams of flight, demanding a vectorial imagination exemplified by the existence of the wind. Compare this to the weightiness of the earthly imagination: "One would never end if one wanted to follow all the dialectics of rock and cloud, if one wanted to live the intumescence of the mountain. In its swellings and its points, in its rounded earth and in its rocks, the mountain is stomach and teeth, it devours the cloudy sky, it swallows the bones of the storm and even the bronze of thunder."[6] And yet, what can be said of the paradoxical case of the Ventoux, where wind and mountain are, in a strange sense, one and the same?

Gustaf Sobin, American born, has lived in the Luberon for the last four decades, just a few kilometers from La Coste, the chateau of the Marquis de Sade.[7] His work—poetry, fiction, and essays, much of which is devoted to Provençal art, landscape, and toponymy—is imbued with the spirit, and the words, of Petrarch, Mallarmé, Heidegger, Blanchot, Char. He writes in a small hut constructed on a hillside near his house, overlooking the valley and the mountains, in full view of Mont Ventoux. He has never mentioned the Ventoux in his writings.

Sobin is a poet of breath and wind, immanance and void. In "The Earth as Air: An Ars Poetica," a poem that is also a poetics, he accepts Stéphane Mallarmé's dictum as his own: "everything I've created has been by *elimination*."[8] For the two poets, this is an extreme statement. The reason Mallarmé gives for this poetic production by reduction is to advance as far as possible into the "Absolute Darkness." But the Ventoux is, after all, the antithesis of all that is mallarméen. He for whom the world exists in order to be transformed into a book, he who loved chiffon and lace, froth and fans, waves and folds, could hardly have been expected to celebrate the Ventoux, a towering, massive, brutal monument of broken stones. But what of Vinturius, that most evanescent of gods? Mallarmé had always preferred the subtle breeze to the violent tempest or the whirlwind, the decorated paper fan to the thunderhead.[9]

The seventh and final poem of Sobin's series, "Odes of Estrangement," concludes:

> . . . oh blown weather
> dis-
>
> banded heart, whatever utters,
> utters nothing, really.   and makes of that
> nothing—lyric—its
> only
> measure.[10]

This is precisely the absolute poetic moment described by Bachelard, where the imagination projects the entirety of being: "When one goes so far, so high, one recognizes oneself to be in the state of *open imagination*. The imagination, whole, greedy for atmospheric realities, doubles each impression with a new image. Being feels itself, as Rilke claimed, on the verge of being written."[11] Here, the "fluid architecture of each given instance" marks, through its turbulent flow, through its unsubstantial substantiality, the origins of the word. This aerian dynamic does not proffer a nihilistic ontology and cannot be reduced to the poetics of negative theology or mysticism, though it may well include them. Rather, it reveals, as Bachelard insists, how the real is a function of the unreal, how reality is but the blockage, the repression, of the imaginary. Such a *pneumatology* is poetically liberatory; and the most extreme state of this atmospheric poetics, of this cosmic dynamics of the imagination, of this psychic pellucidity, is that of the tempest: "It seems that the immense void, by suddenly finding an action, becomes a particularly clear image of cosmic anger. One may say that the furious wind is the symbol of *pure anger,* of anger without object, without pretext."[12] The mistral—that wind which drives humans and animals mad—is the hyperbolic instantiation of this cosmic anger, and the highest peak of the Ventoux, the Col des Tempêtes, is where the mistral blows the strongest. Tales of the mistral are legendary. Sobin recounts the incident of the shepherd who, in the midst of a furious mistral, leads his flock to a pond; the sheep stand there, frozen, looking into the water. He then begins the brutal gesture of raising his whip . . . only to strike the water so that the sheep recognize it, and drink. In another incident, witnessed by Sobin, the mistral twice blows off a local farmer's hat; after the third time, he nails the hat to a tree and blasts it with his shotgun. This anger-provoking wind, this wrathful wind, is like a god: born from itself, invisible, destructive, everywhere and nowhere. But it is like a foreign god, a stranger, unintelligible, disquieting. It infiltrates the meridional regions with currents originating in the septentrional ones, contaminating the *here* with the *elsewhere*. It is such xenophobic fear that constitutes one of the cohesive elements of all locale, but it is precisely this anxiety which must be overcome for culture to exist. For the mistral—which in the popular imagination is part of the essence of Provence—comes from the north, the point of the compass loathed by Petrarch, the region antipodal and antipathetic to the land of the Felibres, a place outside the Mediterranean imagination. This is why it is hated. But there is an extraordinary irony here, since the mistral—however immateral, however furious—is an ever present sign of transcendence, while the Ventoux—however massive, however severe—disappears each time it it promises to become a symbol. Yet after all, these are but two sides of the same being, *Vinturius-Mistral* and *Vinturius-Ventoux,* a god divided—not unlike Dionysus, that other duplicitous outsider, split into *Dionysus Baccheios* and *Dionysus Katharsios,* the former bringing misunderstanding, drunkenness, delirium, madness, murder, the latter offering benevolent catharsis, integration, wholeness, purification.[13] To neglect the rites of either manifestation of the god is to portend the worst. Paradoxically, in the Vaucluse, the foreign wind becomes localized, and the native mountain estranged. For in fact, all locality, all regionality, all nationality, is composed not only of what is common, but also of what is strange, foreign, other. To accept this fact is to understand that inspiration is the infusion of what we do not already know, of what we can never possess, of what takes us beyond ourselves. *Inspiration is disruption, dispossession, dislocation. Inspiration is, in the literal sense of the word, ecstasy.* That is why we read poetry. That is why inspiration is a wind. That is why Mont Ventoux is prodigious.

The mistral, like all wind, is an active psychological and metaphysical principle. It is also a metaphor of poetic inspiration. Bachelard writes: "The *poetic breath,* before being a metaphor, is a reality that one may find in the life of the poem if one wished to follow the lessons of the *material aerian imagination.* And if one paid more attention to poetic exuberance, to all the forms of the pleasure of speaking, softly, rapidly, screaming, murmuring, psalmodizing . . . one would discover an incredible plurality of poetic breaths."[14] And yet, how many would truly choose the mistral, in all its force, as the source of their poetic imagination? How many would desire an inspiration, however fecund, that would drive them mad? Sobin is surely inspired by Bachelard. Might we not also surmise that to some extent he is also inspired—perhaps in the literal, ancient sense of the term—by the mistral, by the Ventoux, by Vinturius? For this poet, the verb is always breath, as he indicates in the poem "Reading Sarcophagi: An Essay":

> wherein "flesh" would find itself inexorably consumed by "word."
>
> and "word"—soon enough—by its own inaudible whisper.[15]

This "inaudible whisper"—Char's "voice so low that no one ever hears it"—is the essence of a certain type of poetry; it is also the breath of life, the nearly silent sounding of the flesh, the site of transcendence (spirit) in immanence (lungs), there where breath conjoins self and world. This "flesh" is later qualified in Sobin's poem by a citation, evincing a certain Heideggerian tenor, taken from Marie-José Mondzain's essay *Image, icône, économie:* "in giving its flesh and figure to the essence of withdrawal, that very invisibility takes possession of all wordly visibilities."[16] What is this flesh; how is it different from the mere biological flesh of our bodies; how is it imbued with transcendence? Perhaps the last writings of Merleau-Ponty can suggest an answer, one congruent with Sobin's poetics. "What we are calling the flesh, this interiorly worked-over mass, has no name in any philosophy [. . .] we must think it [. . .] as an element, as the concrete emblem of a general manner of Being."[17] Like the ancient elements—earth, air, fire, water—the flesh is not of stable form; it is protean, polyvalent, polymorphic, in never-ending metamorphosis. The "flesh" does not correspond either to a physical system or to a metaphysical, ontotheological concept of Being, where there exists an ultimate equivalence of Spirit and Being, thought and thing, truth and reality. The flesh bears no such adequation or closure; it is openness to Being, the ineluctable intertwining of the visible and the invisible. The flesh is Being in perpetual incompletion, a dual movement of possession and dispossession, of belief and doubt. Isn't this antinomy precisely the meaning of paradox, of dialectic, where opposites merge to generate new thought? The flesh is life as paradox, the very structure of the openness of thought.

Integral to Merleau-Ponty's philosophy is the notion of the phenomenological *horizon:* "a new type of being, a being by porosity, pregnancy, or generality, and he before whom the horizon opens is caught up, included within it."[18] It is not by accident that this new ontological terminology centers on a mixed metaphor, of landscape and body, since the open horizon is precisely where the flesh obtains its "adhesion to Being,"[19] where the sensuous, sensual matter of our bodies joins the flesh of Being. This adhesion is structured differently for each and every person, delineated by endlessly shifting trajectories of the gaze and traced by endless, labyrinthine routes traversing the world. "My visible is nowise my 'representation,' but flesh," a perpetual interchange and reversibility between visibility and the visible, body and world, viewer and viewpoint, touching and touched, the visible and the invisible.[20] This is not a theory of transcendence in immanence, but rather of the abolition of the differentiation between innateness and exteriority. The flesh is polyvalent and polymorphic, where sublimation exists through the self-reflexive process of a sort of ontological narcissism, the folding over of thought and flesh upon themselves as the basis of all self-consciousness.

Extrapolating from Merleau-Ponty as well as from Sobin, we might insist that all *genius loci* is *genius locutionis,* the spirit of place is always manifested as a speaking subject. But as we have already seen, every *place* is never only neutral *space,* precisely because it is imbued with *elsewhere,* and sometimes even with *nowhere.* Every space includes a part of *utopia,* in the literal sense of the word. Sobin:

> sublunar, subliminal, nothing's written, in effect, that's not underwritten:
> no world, in effect, that's not—ultimately—underworld.[21]

Language perpetually articulates concept and affect, object and subject, thing and ephemera, space and time. These considerations might be synthesized to present a schematization for a new poetics, one where sublimation is always, in every word and every act, contemporaneous and commensurate with desublimation.

Sublimation: the object disappears
for sign and symbol to exist.
transcendence
divine pneuma
spirit
wind
breath
immanence
Desublimation: the sign is transformed,
deformed into breath and body.

Such is a metaphysics ruled by the trope of the oxymoron, the contradiction in terms, the paradox. But this contradiction is governed by the ratio of degrees of sublimation and desublimation, which changes according to psychological and historical imperatives. Whence the significance of the title, *The Earth as Air,* whence the profound bond between the Ventoux and the Sorgue, the Ventoux and the mistral, Ventoux and Vinturius. *The very existence of Mont Ventoux is an allegory of the structure of poetry, of symbolism itself.* It leads us to the limits of the iconoclastic imagination, where, as Bachelard writes of the violent wind—and we may claim, mutatis mutandis, of the relation between the mistral and the Ventoux—we find that, "on the one hand, a strong will attached to nothing, and on the other, an imagination without any figure, support one another."[22] In another context, Hubert Damisch, in *Théorie du nuage,* shows how such an iconographic fluidity (and not iconophobia, as other commentators might claim)—a fortiori present in the representation of clouds—is precisely what is at stake in modenism: "There where painters of other times sought stability, permanence, clarity, the modern spectator is invited to be satisfied with obscurity, the ephemeral, change, and to derive the greatest satisfaction and learning from what is least easily fixed and understood: the wind, lighting, the shadows of clouds, etc."[23] Such is the materialization of Shakespeare's "far-off mountains turned into clouds" from *A Midsummer Night's Dream;* such is Sobin's "fluid architecture of each given instance."

Sobin offers a key to his poetics in another citation from Mondzain: "that which allows us to see goes on creating, within each of us, a desire to apprehend that very invisibility."[24] Again, Merleau-Ponty: "The invisible is *there* without being an *object,* it is pure transcendence, without an ontic mask. And the 'visibles' themselves, in the last analysis, they too are only centered on a nucleus of absence."[25] Until the advent of the Jewish god, unheard of was the deity that didn't appear behind an "ontic mask." Whence the uniqueness, the poetic appropriateness, of Vinturius, that rare divine manifestation of "pure transcendence without an ontic mask." What better emblem for poetry! "The invisible is *there* without being an *object,*" and as such, argues Merleau-Ponty, "one cannot see it there and every effort to *see it there* makes it disappear, but it is *in the line* of the visible, it is its virtual focus, it is inscribed within it (in filigree)."[26] Doesn't this explain what Handke saw in the genius of Cézanne, specifically to have made visible that fracture on the slopes of the Montagne Sainte-Victoire, to have revealed the fissure which was to become the guiding pivot or axis of Handke's thought? Doesn't this explain what attracted Char to the writing of Heidegger, precisely to have seen in those *Holzwege* of the Black Forest, those sinuous logging trails that lead nowhere, the very structure of philosophical meditation? Isn't this the genius that Sobin sees in Mallarmé's "thin, pale line," the very path of renewing French poetry by twisting and distending the line of alexandrine verse around the void? Might this not be the essence of Sobin's own verse, evincing an iconography and an epistemology worthy of the Ventoux itself?:

'a traced erasure,' you'd once called it. a semiotics, finally, without signs.
as the road, just under, broke, now, into gravel, rubble, dune.[27]

Whence the perennial and inexorable disappearances of Mont Ventoux (gravel, rubble, dune): in mystic vision, religious syncretism, violent attack, blinding fog, poetic metaphor. However often it disappears, it nevertheless refuses to become a symbol: this is the singularity of Mont Ventoux, this is why it is, in a very broad sense of the term, supernatural. The literary history of Mont Ventoux, and its eternal resistance to representation, may well be summed up by Merleau-Ponty's more general observation about the invisible: "one cannot see it there and every effort to *see it there* makes it disappear." Mont Ventoux is not a metaphor, but rather *the metaphor of metaphors, the very allegory of thought.*

Bachelard: "the wind menaces and roars, but takes on form only if it encounters dust: visible, it becomes an impoverished misery."[28] The power of the wind is in its invisible dynamics; once visible, it is an object of derision. Merleau-Ponty: "in the visible there is never anything but ruins of the spirit."[29] Sobin, writing in "Towards the Blanched Alphabets" of the weather that comes from the west, bearing sound that "arrives with its scooped hollows":

. . . there, in those
late
landscapes, that
vaporous ground: grammar's

ultimate retreat.[30]

"Vaporous ground" is but a synonym of "earth as air," which in our context translates into *mountain as wind:* Vinturius. Neither mysticism nor iconoclasm, the lines cited from Bachelard, Merleau-Ponty, Sobin reveal the ontological conditions that permit not only poetry, but thought itself, to exist. These are philosophers who do not require the gods, but who always marvel at their presence.

"I'm a New Yorker." This phrase, or indeed any linking of identity to place, has always seemed suspect to me. I have always related identity—the little of which I am conscious and wish to assume, beyond my identification with my writing—to displacement. My parents were deracinated, having lost everything and suffered the worst in the Holocaust that swept Europe near mid-century. They met and married in a DP (displaced person) camp in Germany after the war. From their tales, my vision of their homes is a mix of nostalgia for their bucolic and small town lives and trembling before a fiery apocalypse well beyond anything imagined by Saint John the Divine or Bosch. I spent my early childhood in the Bronx, and my first impressions of landscape alternated between pleasant strolls in Cretona Park, then a modest but charming public garden, and the vision of that titanic gash in front of our apartment house which ineradicably scarred the neighborhood, indeed the entire borough: a chasm that was to become, in one of Robert Moses's many coercive, brutal, megalomaniacal intrusions on New York's cityscape and landscape, the Cross Bronx Expressway. Both sites had their attractions and their predicaments. I was torn between the garden and the abyss. Many years later, my discovery of Thoreau—who well understood the place of human violence, then manifested by the railroad, in the virgin forest—brought some solace. Having lived all my life in or around New York, I eventually chose Paris as my second city (to perpetually travel between one "city of lights" and another). Perhaps in affinity with Poe and Mallarmé, the light I prefer is artificial, or at least attenuated; I do not share Mistral's eminently Provençal motto, "lou soleu me fai cantar" *(the sun makes me sing). I am only happy in shadow. It wasn't until a few years ago that I discovered my landscape of predilection: the Monts d'Aubrac. These desolate, rock-incrusted, rolling low mountains of the sparsely populated central region of the Massif Central offer vast horizons cut into abstract patterns by the* drailles*—trails lined with low stone walls and fences that cut across the pastures—which always seem to lead to either nowhere or directly to the cloud-strewn sky. The house I rent there bears the sort of equivocation that well suits my hesitations about identity: built in the last century, it was first a famhouse, then the village school, later a café, and finally a private residence, now a writer's den, given over to someone doubly foreign: from Paris, from New York. Perhaps a brief anecdote might explain my choice of landscape. In what is now the hamlet of Aubrac—where the departments of the Lozère, the Aveyron and the*

Cantal meet—a vast religious complex, the Hospice de Notre-Dame des Pauvres, was built in the twelfth century to shelter pilgrims on their way to Santiago de Compostela. Today, only a tower, a small church, and a cemetery remain. Over the portal to the main entrance were written the words "In loco horroris et vastae solitudinis."

I met Gustaf Sobin for the first time at his home in the Luberon on 28 November 2000. From his writing hut, Mont Ventoux was dazzlingly and gloriously visible on the horizon.[31] *In front of his house stands a seventeenth-century* borie, *a small, domed, dry stone shepherd's shelter. In March 1993, while doing repairs on this structure, he discovered a damaged, rectangular chunk of conchitic limestone that had obviously been used some time in the distant past to repair a fault in the borie. This stone bears the dedication:* "Vinturi. . . ." *The rest of the inscription is illegible. This fragment is the upper part of an altar of the god Vinturius, the top of which was slightly hollowed out, thus creating a miniature hearth, a* foculus, *that point of concentration in which oblations to the god were burnt: wine, honey, myrrh, aromatic herbs. The smoke from this tiny altar would, ironically, almost make Vinturius visible for but a moment, rising in the fumes of the very offerings sent up to him, like a miniature djinn from a magic bottle. Visible, but hardly distinguishable.*[32] *I share a destiny with the Ventoux, with Vinturius, a destiny of dispossession and deracination, ephemerality and transition, a poetic destiny that Sobin paradoxically characterizes as one where, ". . . we articulate* away *from ourselves in a continuous elision* towards.*"*[33] Per fumum, *through smoke.*

In this shattered fragment, I had found the altar of the god without altars. Its sacred smoke no longer wafts in the mistral, a "fluid architecture of each given instance." It is no longer his altar, but not yet his tomb.

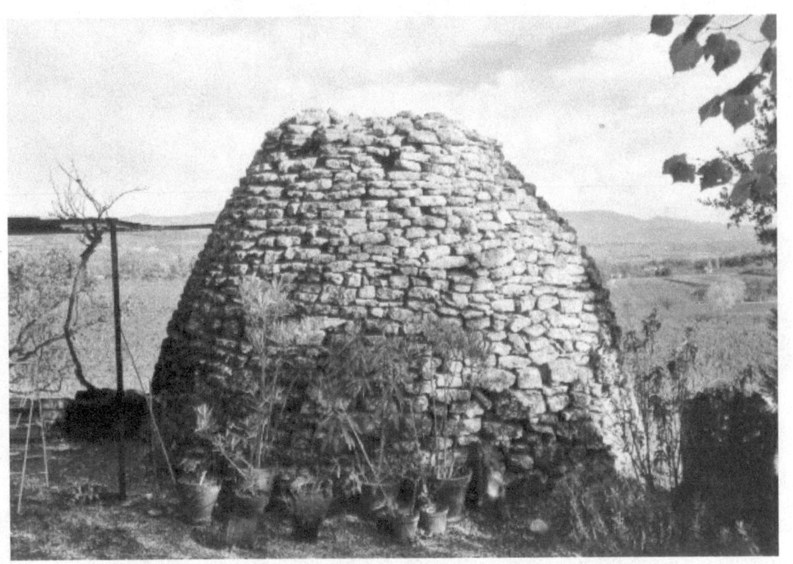

FIGURE 14. Borie.

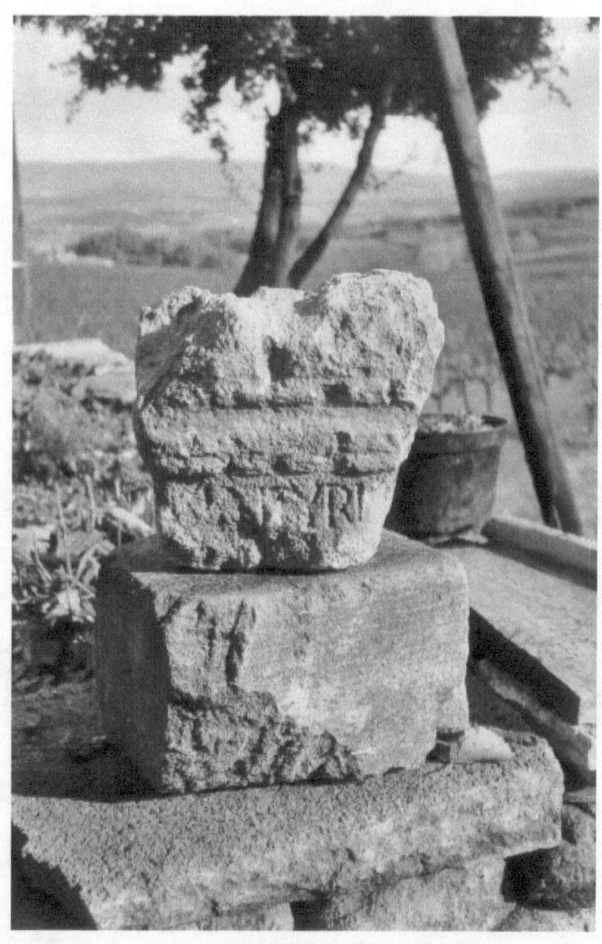

FIGURE 15. Altar of Vinturius.

Notes

All translations are by the author unless otherwise indicated.

PREFACE

1. Richard F. Burton, "Terminal Essay" (1886) in *The Book of the Thousand Nights and a Night,* vol. 10 (privately printed by the Burton Club in the USA, n.d.), 102.

I. ASCENT

1. Francesco Petrarca (Petrarch), *Rerum familiarium libri,* vols. 1–8 [Letters on Family Matters], trans. Aldo S. Bernardo (Albany: State University of New York Press, 1975), 173.

2. There is record of another ascent of Mont Ventoux between the time of the shepherd's and Petrarch's climb: the Parisian scholastic Jean Buridan climbed the mountain some time before 1334. One wonders whether Petrarch's shepherd had also encountered Buridan, and tried to dissuade him from his climb. Mentioned in Marjorie Hope Nicolson, *Mountain Gloom and Mountain Glory: The Development of the Aesthetics of the Infinite* (Ithaca, NY: Cornell University Press, 1959), 49n. It should be noted that Nicolson's extraordinary book bears no mention of Mont Ventoux other than that of Petrarch's letter.

3. *Rerum familiarium libri,* vols. 1–8: 174–75.

4. Ibid., 176.

5. Ibid., 177.

6. Ibid., 178.

7. It should be mentioned that the first post-classic pictorial representation of a landscape is almost exactly contemporaneous with Petrarch's letter: Ambrogio Lorenzetti's fresco "The Good Government," painted between 1337 and 1339 for the Palazzo Pubblico in Siena.

8. Derek Pearsall and Elizabeth Salter, *Landscapes and Seasons of the Medieval World* (Toronto: University of Toronto Press, 1973), 42–43.

9. Maurice Merleau-Ponty, *The Visible and the Invisible,* trans. Alphonso Lingis (Evanston: Northwestern University Press, 1968), 270.

10. This is why the poem of the great Japanese poet, Matsuo Bashō, in which Mount Fuji disappears is so striking:

In a way
It was fun
Not to see Mount Fuji
In foggy rain.

It also explains the poignancy of his observation, as he took to the road to begin his long journey north, that, "The faint shadow of Mount Fuji and the cherry blossoms of Ueno and Yanaka were bidding me a last farewell." Matsuo Bashō, *The Narrow Road to the Deep North,* trans. Nobuyuki Yuasa (New York: Penguin, 1966), 51 and 98.

11. Francesco Petrarch, *The Life of Solitude* [*De vita solitaria,* 1346], trans. Jacob Zeitlin (Urbana: University of Illinois Press, 1924), 298. This book abounds in references to mountains: those frequented by Saints Augustine, Francis, Benoît, and Martin, as well as Moses, Seneca, Dante. However, it is not the Ventoux, but rather the Atlas Mountains (the scene of his epic poem, *Africa*) that is so honored. See Francesco Petrarch, *Petrarch's Secret* [*Secretum;* 134], trans. William H. Draper (London: Chatto and Windus, 1949; reprinted Norwood Editions, 1976), 92. On the relations between the pagan and Christian traditions of mountaintop paradises and holy caverns, see Chris Fitter, *Poetry, Space, Landscape* (Cambridge: Cambridge University Press, 1995), 114–16.

12. *Petrarch's Secret,* 92.

13. Ibid., 21.

14. Saint Augustine, *Confessions,* trans. R. S. Pine-Coffin (New York: Penguin, 1961), 216.

15. Ibid., 171.

16. Ibid., 172.

17. Ibid., 178. The biblical source is *Romans* 13:13, 14.

18. Ibid., 197.

19. Ibid., 198.

20. Ibid., 216.

21. *Poetry, Space, Landscape,* 118.

22. See *Mountain Gloom and Mountain Glory,* 72–112.

23. Augustine, *Confessions,* 78.

24. Francesco Petrarca (Petrarch), *Rerum familiarium libri,* vols. 9–16 [Letters on Family Matters], trans. Aldo S. Bernardo (Baltimore: Johns Hopkins University Press, 1982), 204.

25. *Confessions,* 215.

26. Ibid., 197.

27. Francesco Petrarch, *Petrarch's Lyric Poems,* trans. and ed. Robert M. Durling (Cambridge, MA: Harvard University Press, 1976), 421. Translation modified.

28. *Rerum familiarium libri,* vols 9–16, 206.

29. For an excellent study of Petrarch's gardens in the broader historic context of the history of landscape, see Gaëtane Lamarche-Vadel, *Jardins secrets de la Renaissance: Des astres, des simples et des prodiges* (Paris: L'Harmattan, 1997), 45–59.

30. "The very looks of the place prompted me to undertake a silvan work, the *Bucolicum carmen,* and the *De vita solitaria.*" Francesco Petrarch, *Rerum senilium libri,* vols. 1–18 [Letters of Old Age], trans. Aldo S. Bernardo, Saul Levin, and Reta A. Bernardo (Baltimore: Johns Hopkins University Press, 1992), 676.

31. Among his many diatribes against Avignon and city life, see especially the already cited letter to Francesco of the Church of the Holy Apostles (*Rerum familiarium libri,* 9–16: 204–6), and the letter of 1373 to Lombardo della Seta (*Rerum senilium libri,* 1–18: 558–68). It should be noted that the frescoes in the Garde Robe of the Palais des Papes in Avignon depict scenes with both garden and forest backgrounds full of flora and fauna, another example of the urban sources of rural imagery.

32. *Rerum familiarium libri,* 1–8: 313.

33. *Life of Solitude,* 290.

34. Ibid., 220.

35. *Petrarch's Lyric Poems,* 459. Translation modified.

36. Cited in Charles-Albert Cingria, *Pétrarque* (1932; Lausanne: L'Age d'Homme, 2003), 111.

37. In an extraordinarily kitsch rendition of the metaphor of the "speaking river," it is not uncommon to find sound and light shows in which, by means of recorded voices, rivers "speak" their own history, as is the case, for example, in the town of Estaing (Aveyron) in the Lot river valley in France. Such contraptions are insufferably ridiculous, and show the extent to which a sense of willful disbelief is needed not only in relation to the acceptance of poetry, but regarding all figures of rhetoric.

38. *Life of Solitude,* 299.

39. See *Poetry, Space, Landscape,* 156–97.

40. For the relation between Petrarch and the troubadors, see Cingria's *Pétrarque*. The biblical model of the *Song of Songs* has always been a source for combining landscape symbolism with erotic body symbolism, and for conflating sacred and profane love.

41. *Rima Sparse* #288, in *Petrarch's Lyric Poems,* 467. Translation modified.

42. *Poetry, Space, Landscape,* 169.

43. *Rerum familiarium libri,* 1–8: 176.

44. *Petrarch's Secret,* 185.

II. DISAPPEARANCE

1. During that time, however, the Ventoux was a site of scientific research: in 1561 the botanist Anguillaria studied its flora; a century later the Platter brothers did the same, publishing the first botanical study of the mountain; and, as might be expected, numerous amateurs and specialist climbed to its peak in attempts to calculate its height. In terms of the sparse iconography of Mont Ventoux, one curious example has been discovered. The Musée de Villeneuve-lès-Avignon possesses a painting of *Le Couronnement de la Vierge* [The Coronation of the Virgin] by Enguerrand Quarton from 1453–54, where the cities of Rome and Jerusalem are actually depictions of Avignon and Villeneuve-lès-Avignon; on the horizon behind

Rome/Avignon rises the unmistakeable silhouette of the Ventoux. I wish to thank Gustaf Sobin for this information.

2. There is no single Provençal language, but rather a vast and more or less continuous spectrum of dialects and patois ranging from northern Italy through the Alps, Provence and Languedoc, through to Catalonia. Though there are major national and regional variants that form determinate linguistic groups within this spectrum, there are also minor but notable differences of vocabulary and pronunciation that often differ between villages situated only a few kilometers apart. France d'oc and France d'oïl (respectively the regions south and north of the Loire valley) merged in the year 1271.

3. Cited in Cingria, *Pétrarque,* 140.

4. Frédéric Mistral, *Calendau* (1866; Barcelona: Edicioun Ramoun Berenguié, 1966), 276. My translation. The other great Félibrist evocation of Mont Ventoux is in Félix Gras, *Li Carbounié* (1876). It should be noted that Jules Michelet, in *La montagne* (1868) never once mentions Mont Ventoux.

5. Frédéric Mistral, *Mémoires et récits* [*Memòri e raconti,* 1906] (Paris and Geneva: Slatkine, 1995), 251.

6. Ibid., 252.

7. Ibid., 259.

8. Jean-Henri Fabre, "Une ascension au mont Ventoux" (excerpted from *Souvenirs entomologiques,* 1879) (Paris: Mercure de France, 1997), 11–12.

9. Edmund Burke, *A Philosophical Enquiry into the Origin of Our Ideas of the Sublime and the Beautiful* (1757; Notre Dame: University of Notre Dame Press, 1958), 129–60. For a detailed history of the theory of the sublime, see *Mountain Gloom and Mountain Glory,* 271–323.

10. *Mountain Gloom and Mountain Glory,* 143.

11. Cited in *Mountain Gloom and Mountain Glory,* 277.

12. Immanuel Kant, *Critique of Judgement,* trans. J. H. Bernard (1790; New York: Hafner, 1972), 100. On the relation between romantic poetry and metaphysics, centered on the work of Wordsworth, see M. H. Abrams, *Natural Supernatural: Tradition and Revolution in Romantic Literature* (New York: W. W. Norton, 1971), especially the chapter entitled "The Theodicy of the Landscape," 97–117.

13. The French spellings are: Calendal, Estérelle, Comte Sévéran. The Provençal for the Ventoux is Le Ventour.

14. *Calendau,* 280.

15. Ibid., 282.

16. Ibid., 280.

17. Ibid., 280.

18. Ibid., 282.

19. Ibid., 284.

20. Ibid., 298.

21. Ibid., 300.

22. Ibid., 278. On the literary structures of the past, see Pascal Quignard, *Dernier royaume II: Sur le jadis* (Paris: Grasset, 2002).

23. The finest biography to date is Jean-Luc Steinmetz, *Stéphane Mallarmé* (Paris: Fayard, 1998); see also the catalogue of the exhibition at the Grand Palais, *Mallarmé 1842–1898: Un destin d'écriture* (Paris: Gallimard/Réunion des Musées Nationaux, 1998). In conversation, Steinmetz confirmed that he found no mention whatsoever of Mont Ventoux in Mallarmé's correspondence or other writings.

24. Stéphane Mallarmé, letter to Théodore Aubanel (16 July 1866), in *Correspondance* (Paris: Gallimard/Folio, 1995), 312. For a detailed account of enunciations from the point of view of the dead in relation to Mallarmé and modernist poetry, see Allen S. Weiss, *Breathless: Sound Recording, Disembodiment, and the Transformation of Lyrical Nostalgia* (Middletown: Wesleyan University Press, 2002), 29–66.

25. Ibid., letter to Henri Cazalis (14 May 1867), 343.

26. Ibid.

27. Ibid., letter to Henri Cazalis (28 April 1866), 297–98.

28. Ibid., letter to Eugène Lefébure (3 May 1868), 384.

29. Ibid., letter to Henri Cazalis (3 April 1870), 470.

30. Stéphane Mallarmé, *Igitur,* in *Oeuvres complètes* (Paris: Gallimard/Pléiade, 1945), 43.

31. *Correspondence,* letter to Villiers de l'Isle-Adam (24 September 1867), 366–67.

32. Jean-Pierre Richard, *L'univers imaginaire de Mallarmé* (Paris: Le Seuil, 1961), 69. Richard cites the poem "Las de l'amer repos" as being of special interest in this regard.

33. The proper verb here is indeed *sublime,* which means to pass directly from a solid to a gaseous state.

34. *Correspondance,* letter to Frédéric Mistral (August 1867), 365. Mention of the bee is another reference to *Calendau,* where the protagonist gathers a huge amount of honey to impress his beloved.

35. Ibid., letter to Eugène Lefébure (3 May 1868), 384–85.

36. See Alain Roger, *Court traité du paysage* (Paris: Gallimard, 1997), 24–30.

37. Richard Sieburth, "Introduction: 'To Set Here the Roads of France,'" in Ezra Pound, *A Walking Tour in Southern France* (New York: New Directions, 1992), xiii–xiv.

38. "Une ascension au mont Ventoux," 18.

39. Ibid., 24.

40. Henry David Thoreau, *The Maine Woods* (1864; New York: Penguin, 1988), 110.

41. Ibid., 84.

42. Ibid., 85.

43. Ibid., 86.

44. See *Mountain Gloom and Mountain Glory,* 34–71.

45. Thomas Burnet, *The Sacred Theory of the Earth* (London, 1684), cited in *Mountain Gloom and Mountain Glory,* 210.

46. *The Maine Woods,* 94. It should be added that this rapt elegy of mountains is quite exceptional in Thoreau's writings. Quite to the contrary—and most to the point of the transcendentalist sensibility, where *all* of nature is a source of inspiration—he claims, in a statement that offers no postlapsarian critique of the earth, "Olympus is but the outside of the earth everywhere." *Walden* (1854; New York: Modern Library, 1950), 76.

47. "Une ascension au Mont Ventoux," 13.

III. METAPHOR

1. René Char, "Le Thor" in *Oeuvres complètes* (Paris: Gallimard/Pléiade, 1983), 239.

2. René Magritte would materialize this metaphor in his painting *Le domaine d'Arnheim* (1949), named after a tale by Edgar Allan Poe. In the painting, the shattered glass of a window offers two vistas upon a mountain

range where a snow-covered peak is presented in the form of an eagle: one through the window itself, and the other in the broken panes of glass lying on the floor of the room.

3. *Calendau,* 284.

4. "Le Thor," 239.

5. Jean-François Lyotard, *Discours, figure* (Paris: Klincksieck, 1974), 289.

6. For an exemplary reading of the complexities of modern rhetoric, see Laurent Jenny, *La parole singulière* (Paris: Belin, 1990), 13–41.

7. It must be noted that the twentieth century, the age of mechanical and electronic reproduction, is a hyperbolically panoptical time: nothing can hide. This is equally true of the Ventoux. Consider a few key phenomena, amongst so many others. The works of a writer like Jean Giono—an author of Provence whose influence extends far beyond that of the Felibres and other regional writers—have spurred immense romantic interest in the region; furthermore, Provence and Tuscany seem to have become ideal destinations for Americans, and the bestseller lists always seem to contain books on both regions; and at least since the postwar presence of Char in the region, the Luberon and the Vaucluse have become favorite sites for secondary residences of the French, as well as many others, to the point that the two major towns near the Ventoux, Bedoin and Malaucène, host a veritable "Who's Who" of Parisian intellectuals. Finally, just to make a quantitative point, it might be added that in the year 2000 the Tour de France included an ascent of Mont Ventoux, as reported in the newspaper *Le Monde* of 13 July 2000; the mountain is referred to as "the terrible Mont Ventoux [. . .] there are only stones, spectators and cars." Two years later, on 21 July 2002, the sports broadcaster of the radio station France Info referred to the Ventoux as an "enigmatic wart upon nature." That day, it is estimated that approximately 300,000 people lined the roads leading to and climbing up the Ventoux to see the race! An article by Julian Barnes in *The New Yorker* (21 and 28 August 2000) describing the same race, proclaims: "When the tree line runs out, there is nothing up there but you and the weather, which is violent and capricious." It has been suggested to me that in fact Mont Ventoux is indelibly marked on the French imagination not at all because of Petrarch's letter, but due rather to the infamous moment, on 13 July 1967, when during the Tour de France the British cyclist Tom Simpson collapsed and died during the ascent of the mountain.

8. Cited in René Char, notes to *La nuit talismanique qui brillait dans son cercle* (1972), in *Oeuvres complètes,* 1385.

9. Gabriel Bounoure, "René Char," *L'Arc,* no. 22 (1963); also cited in René Char, *Oeuvres complètes,* 1179. In fact, during Char's transfer from the

Alps to North Africa, the Mont Ventoux served as a clandestine landing strip for an intermediary stage of the flight. Rather than a feeling of homecoming, Char was vexed by this departure. "The crest of Mont Ventoux kept upon its slopes a frozen covering of clouds, clouds that had ceased to live." René Char, cited in Marie-Claude Char, ed., *René Char: Faire du chemin avec . . .* (Avignon: Palais des Papes, 1990), 131–32.

10. Ibid., 1179.

11. Ibid., 1179.

12. René Char, "La Sorgue," in *Oeuvres complètes,* 274

13. René Char, "Les premiers instants," in *Oeuvres complètes,* 275. This poem is preceded by a hymn to the river in question, "La Sorgue."

14. Paul Veyne, *René Char en ses poèmes* (Paris: Gallimard, 1990), 36.

15. Ibid., 68. Given that Char's work is exceedingly sparse in citations, it might also be of interest to note that the early collection of poems, *Moulin premier* (1935–36), bears as its epigraph a citation from Fabre: "What is needed here, a contradiction without exit, what is needed here, totally necessary, is the immobility of death and the freshness of the entrails of life." *Oeuvres complètes,* 60. Another collection, *Le soleil des eaux* (1946), has as one of its epigraphs part of a letter from Petrarch, vaunting the simplicity, isolation, and freedom felt in his "asylum," the Vaucluse. *Oeuvres complètes,* 938.

16. René Char, "Même si . . ." in *Le nu perdu* (1964–70), in *Oeuvres complètes,* 467. Char was one of Heidegger's hosts during the time of his seminars in France, and in turn Char was considered by the philospher to be one of the major contemporary French poets.

17. René Char, "Peu à peu, puis un vin siliceux," in *La nuit talismanique,* in *Oeuvres complètes,* 494.

18. René Char, "À faulx contente" (1972), in *Oeuvres complètes,* 783.

19. René Char, "Contrevenir," in *Oeuvres complètes,* 413.

20. Maurice Blanchot, "La bête de Lascaux," *L'Herne,* no. 15 (Paris, 1971), an issue devoted to René Char, partially reprinted in *Oeuvres complètes,* 1176–77.

21. Pierre Michon, *Trois auteurs* (Lagrasse: Verdier, 1997), 51.

22. Ibid., 65–66.

23. *The Visible and the Invisible,* 125.

24. Charles Rostaing, *Essai sur la toponymie en Provence* (Paris, 1950).

25. Camille Jullian, "Le Mont Sainte-Victoire et Deus Vintur," *Revue des Études anciennes,* vol. 1 (1899), 50–57; cited in André Bouyala d'Arnaud, "Toponymie et histoire de la montagne Sainte-Victoire," *Revue de Philosophie et d'Histoire* (1958), 36.

26. In fact, there are no underground currents connecting these mountains with Fontaine-de-Vaucluse, whose true source is to be found on the Plateau d'Albion.

27. Marjorie Leach, *A Guide to the Gods* (Santa Barbara: ABC-CLIO, 1992). On the names of winds, see the marvelous book by Honorin Victoire, *Petite Encyclopédie des Vents de France* (Paris: J. C. Lattès, 2001).

28. Michel Clerc, *La Bataille d'Aix,* 272; cited in "Toponymie et histoire de la montagne Sainte-Victoire," 36.

29. Millin, *Voyages dans les départements du midi de la France,* vol. 3 (Paris: Imprimerie Impériale, 1801–1807), 113–14; cited in "Toponymie et histoire de la montagne Sainte-Victoire," 42.

30. Peter Handke, *The Lesson of Mont Sainte-Victoire* (1980), trans. Ralph Manheim (New York: Farrar, Straus, Giroux, 1985), 145.

31. Ibid., 146.

32. Ibid., 159.

33. Ibid., 156.

34. Ibid., 160.

35. Michel Chaillou, *Le sentiment géographique* (Paris: Gallimard, 1976), 171–72.

36. Robert Smithson, "A Sedimentation of the Mind: Earth Projects" (1968), in *Robert Smithson: The Collected Writings* (Berkeley: University of California Press, 1996), 107.

37. *Lesson of Mont Sainte-Victoire,* 195.

38. Ibid., 197.

39. Ibid., 198.

40. René Char, "Les Dentelles de Montmirail," in the collection *La Parole en archipel* (1952–60), *Oeuvres complètes,* 413 (Char's italics). Paul Veyne mentions that he brought the archaeological discovery of the trumpets to Char's attention in 1960, and that the archaeologist Jacques Jully had also spoken of them to the poet; see Veyne, *René Char en ses poèmes,* 68, and J. J. Jully, "Deux trompettes en terre cuite du Mont Ventoux," *OGAM,* vol. 13,

nos. 3–4, 427–30. A fragment of a similar trumpet also existed in the collection of Mistral.

41. René Char, "À faulx contente" (1972), in *Oeuvres complètes,* 783.

42. *René Char en ses poèmes,* 243. It appears that Mont Ventoux was, in fact, much more present in Char's life than his writings would have one believe. I was told by a French poet who knew Char towards the end of his life that he regularly spent parts of his summers at the foot of the Ventoux, at Le Barroux and Blauvac, a fact apparently not reported in his biographies.

43. Ibid., 409.

44. Ibid., 505. One of Char's rare references to Mont Ventoux was in a short piece entitled "La Provence point oméga," written in 1965 as a protest against the installation of nuclear missiles in Haute-Provence: "Ventoux truffles, vines from everywhere, wild mushrooms, today's apples, abridged produce, Provençal peaches, all wounded to death will be the earth that you produce." But here we also find an indirect, though telling, reference to the Sorgue, for he claims that "All roads would lead to the Plateau d'Albion," which is, after all, the actual source of that river. *Oeuvres complètes,* 1312.

IV. BREATH

1. Gustaf Sobin, *Luminous Debris: Reflecting on Vestige in Provence and Languedoc* (Berkeley: University of California Press, 1999), 141–42.

2. "Les Dentelles de Montmirail," *Oeuvres complètes,* 413.

3. Gaston Bachelard, *L'air et les songes: Essai sur l'imagination du mouvement* (Paris: José Corti, 1943), 12.

4. See Allen S. Weiss, "Dematerialization and Iconoclasm," in Allen S. Weiss, *Unnatural Horizons: Paradox and Contradiction in Landscape Architecture* (New York: Princeton Architectural Press, 1998), 44–63; and Hervé Chandès, ed., *Azur* (Paris: Fondation Cartier, 1993).

5. *L'air et les songes,* 195.

6. Gaston Bachelard, *La terre et les rêveries de la volonté* (Paris: José Corti, 1947), 186.

7. The Ventoux is also fully visible from Sade's chateau. However, D. A. F. Sade never mentioned it in his writings. Sade's uncle, the Abbé de Sade, wrote what still remains one of the key texts on Petrarch, *Mémoires pour une vie de Pétrarque.* The Sade family interest in Petrarch was in no small part due to the fact that Petrarch's beloved was Laura di Sade. Char

was early on influenced by Sade, and published an "Hommage à D. A. F. Sade" in the second volume of *Le Surréalisme au service de la révolution* (1930); this is in part a critique of idealism, valorizing a Sade who, "finally saved love from the mud of the sky." Char, *Oeuvres complètes,* 1359.

8. Gustaf Sobin, "The Earth as Air: An Ars Poetica," in *The Earth as Air* (New York: New Directions, 1984), 89. The Mallarmé citation comes from a letter to Eugène Lefébure dated 27 May 1867, in *Correspondance,* 348–49. See *L'univers imaginaire de Mallarmé,* 183–87. Sobin's poem bears as its epigraph a citation from Mallarmé; another of his collections of poetry, *Voyaging Portraits* (New York: New Directions, 1988), published in the year of René Char's death, is dedicated to this poet-neighbor.

9. But there is perhaps another reason, the most profound, for this avoidance. After his crisis of 1866, the most poignant and wrenching moment of Mallarmé's life was the death of his young son Anatole in 1879. He had planned to write a memorial poem, "Tombeau pour Anatole," for which there remains only a set of notes. In a thought that assimilates the double tragedy of nature, the daily sunset and the autumnal fall into night—the very core of the question of being and nothingness—with the death of his son, he writes: "Soleil couché et vent or parti, et vent de *rien qui souffle* (là, le néant moderne)?" [Sunset and gold wind departed, and wind of *nothing that blows* (there, the modern nothingness)?] The modern icon of death is invisible, the wind of nothingness.

10. Gustaf Sobin, "Seventh Ode: The Relics," in the series "Odes of Estrangement," in *Breaths' Burials* (New York: New Directions, 1995), 99.

11. *L'air et les songes,* 13.

12. Ibid., 256.

13. Marcel Detienne, *Dionysos à ciel ouvert* (Paris: Hachette, 1986), 42.

14. *L'air et les songes,* 271.

15. Gustaf Sobin, "Reading Sarcophagi: An Essay," in *Towards the Blanched Alphabets* (Jersey City: Talisman House, 1998), 87.

16. Marie-José Mondzain, *Image, icône, économie* (Paris: Le Seuil, 1996), cited in *Towards the Blanched Alphabets,* 88.

17. *Visible and the Invisible,* 147. See Allen S. Weiss, "Merleau-Ponty's Concept of the 'Flesh' as Libido Theory," *SubStance,* no. 30 (1981), 85–95.

18. *Visible and the Invisible,* 149.

19. Ibid., 270. For a study of landscape inspired by Merleau-Ponty's phenomenology, see Allen S. Weiss, *Mirrors of Infinity: The French Formal Gar-*

den and 17th-Century Metaphysics (New York: Princeton Architectural Press, 1995), 32–51. Also of interest are three books on the phenomenology of place and space by Edward S. Casey, *Getting Back into Place* (Bloomington: Indiana University Press, 1993); *The Fate of Place* (Berkeley: University of California Press, 1997); and *Representing Place* (Berkeley: University of California Press, 2002).

20. *Visible and the Invisible,* 274.

21. Gustaf Sobin, "Premises," in *Towards the Blanched Alphabets,* 8.

22. *L'air et les songes,* 256.

23. Hubert Damisch, *Théorie du nuage : Pour une histoire de la peinture* (Paris: Le Seuil, 1972), 259.

24. Cited in *Towards the Blanched Alphabets,* 105.

25. *Visible and the Invisible,* 229.

26. Ibid., 215.

27. Gustaf Sobin, "Late Bronze, Early Iron: A Journey Book," in *Towards the Blanched Alphabets,* 29.

28. *L'air et les songes,* 257.

29. *Visible and the Invisible,* 180.

30. *Towards the Blanched Alphabets,* 63.

31. I first read of Mont Ventoux in Petrarch's letter, and first saw the mountain in the 1980s, while a guest at the home—situated at the foot of the mountain's southern slope—of the phenomenological philosopher Marc Richir and his wife France, a novelist. Perhaps apposite to my reflections is the fact that Marc Richir wrote, some years later, a book entitled *La naissance des dieux* (Paris: Hachette, 1995.) Need I add that in this work there is no mention of Vinturius?

32. On ritual sacrifice and oblation, in a very different, but not unrelated, context, see Marcel Detienne, *Les Jardins d'Adonis : La mythologie des aromates en Grèce* (Paris: Gallimard, 1972), and Marcel Detienne and Jean-Pierre Vernant, *La Cuisine du sacrifice en pays grec* (Paris: Gallimard, 1979).

33. "The Earth as Air: An Ars Poetica," 89.

Select Bibliography

Abrams, M. H. *Natural Supernatural: Tradition and Revolution in Romantic Literature.* New York: W. W. Norton, 1971.

d'Arnauld, André Bouyala. "Toponymie et histoire de la montagne Sainte-Victoire." *Revue de Philosophie et d'Histoire* (1958).

Saint Augustine. *Confessions*. Trans. R. S. Pine-Coffin. New York: Penguin, 1961.

Bachelard, Gaston. *L'air et les songes : Essai sur l'imagination du mouvement.* Paris: José Corti, 1943.

———. *L'eau et les rêves : Essai sur l'imagination de la matière.* Paris: José Corti, 1942.

———. *La terre et les rêveries de la volonté.* Paris: José Corti, 1947.

———. *La terre et les rêveries du repos.* Paris: José Corti, 1948.

Bashō, Matsuo. *The Narrow Road to the Deep North.* Trans. Nobuyuki Yuasa. New York: Penguin, 1966.

Blanchot, Maurice. "La bête de Lascaux," *L'Herne,* no. 15 (Paris, 1971).

Burke, Edmund. *A Philosophical Enquiry into the Origin of Our Ideas of the Sublime and the Beautiful.* 1757. Reprint, Notre Dame: University of Notre Dame Press, 1958.

Burton, Richard F. "Terminal Essay" (1886). In *The Book of the Thousand Nights and a Night,* vol. 10. Privately printed by the Burton Club in the USA, n.d.

Casey, Edward S. *The Fate of Place*. Berkeley: University of California Press, 1997.

———. *Getting Back into Place*. Bloomington: Indiana University Press, 1993.

———. *Representing Place*. Berkeley: University of California Press, 2002.

Chaillou, Michel. *Le sentiment géographique*. Paris: Gallimard, 1976.

Chandès, Hervé, ed. *Azur*. Paris: Fondation Cartier, 1993.

Char, Marie-Claude, ed. *René Char : Faire du chemin avec. . . .* Avignon: Palais des Papes, 1990.

Char, René. *Oeuvres complètes*. Paris: Gallimard/Pléiade, 1983.

Cingria, Charles-Albert. *Pétrarque*. 1932. Reprint, Lausanne: L'Age d'Homme, 2003.

Damisch, Hubert. *Théorie du nuage : Pour une histoire de la peinture*. Paris: Le Seuil, 1972.

Detienne, Marcel. *Dionysos à ciel ouvert*. Paris: Hachette, 1986.

———. *Les Jardins d'Adonis : La mythologie des aromates en Grèce*. Paris: Gallimard, 1972.

Detienne, Marcel, and Jean-Pierre Vernant. *La Cuisine du sacrifice en pays grec*. Paris: Gallimard, 1979.

Fitter, Chris. *Poetry, Space, Landscape*. Cambridge: Cambridge University Press, 1995.

Handke, Peter. *Die Lehre der Sainte Victoire*. Frankfurt: Suhrkamp, 1980. Trans. Ralph Mannheim. *The Lesson of Mont Sainte-Victoire* (New York: Farrar, Straus, Giroux, 1985).

Hunt, John Dixon. *Greater Perfection: The Practice of Garden Theory*. Philadelphia: University of Pennsylvania Press, 1999.

Jenny, Laurent. *La parole singulière*. Paris: Belin, 1990.

Jullian, Camille. "Le Mont Sainte-Victoire et Deus Vintur," *Revue des Études anciennes*, vol. 1 (1899).

Jully, J. J. "Deux trompettes en terre cuite du Mont Ventoux," *OGAM*, vol. 13, nos. 3–4.

Kant, Immanuel. *Kritik der Urteilskraft*. Berlin and Liebau: 1790. Trans J. H. Bernard. *Critique of Judgement* (New York: Hafner, 1972).

Lamarche-Vadel, Gaëtane. *Jardins secrets de la Renaissance : Des astres, des simples et des prodiges*. Paris: L'Harmattan, 1997.

Leach, Marjorie. *A Guide to the Gods*. Santa Barbara: ABC-CLIO, 1992.

Lyotard, Jean-François. *Discours, figure*. Paris: Klincksieck, 1974.

Mallarmé, Stéphane. *Correspondance*. Paris: Gallimard/Folio, 1995.

———. *Oeuvres complètes*. Paris: Gallimard/Pléiade, 1945.

Merleau-Ponty, Maurice. *Le Visible et l'Invisible*. Paris: Gallimard, 1964. Trans. Alphonso Lingis. *The Visible and the Invisible* (Evanston: Northwestern University Press, 1968).

Michon, Pierre. *Trois auteurs*. Lagrasse: Verdier, 1997.

Mistral, Frédéric. *Calendau*. 1866. Reprint, Barcelona: Edicioun Ramoun Berenguié, 1966.

———. *Mémoires et récits [Memòri e raconti]*. 1906. Reprint, Paris and Geneva: Slatkine, 1995.

Mondzain, Marie-José. *Image, icône, économie*. Paris: Le Seuil, 1996.

Nicolson, Marjorie Hope. *Mountain Gloom and Mountain Glory: The Development of the Aesthetics of the Infinite*. Ithaca, NY: Cornell University Press, 1959.

Pearsall, Derek, and Elizabeth Salter. *Landscapes and Seasons of the Medieval World*. Toronto: University of Toronto Press, 1973.

Petrarch, Francesco. *De vita solitaria* (1346). Trans. Jacob Zeitlin. *The Life of Solitude* (Urbana: University of Illinois Press, 1924).

———. *Petrarch's Lyric Poems*. Trans. and ed. Robert M. Durling. Cambridge, MA: Harvard University Press, 1976.

———. *Secretum* (1347). Trans. William H. Draper. *Petrarch's Secret* (London: Chatto and Windus, 1949. Reprint: Norwood Editions, 1976).

———. *Rerum familiarium libri,* vols. 1–8 [Letters on Family Matters]. Trans. Aldo S. Bernardo. Albany: State University of New York Press, 1975.

———. *Rerum familiarium libri,* vols 9–16 [Letters on Family Matters]. Trans. Aldo S. Bernardo. Baltimore: Johns Hopkins University Press, 1982.

———. *Rerum senilium libri,* vols. 1–18 [Letters of Old Age]. Trans. Aldo S. Bernardo, Saul Levin, and Reta A. Bernardo. Baltimore: Johns Hopkins University Press, 1992.

Quignard, Pascal. *Dernier royaume II : Sur le jadis*. Paris: Grasset, 2002.

Richard, Jean-Pierre. *L'univers imaginaire de Mallarmé*. Paris: Le Seuil, 1961.

Richir, Marc. *La naissance des dieux*. Paris: Hachette, 1995.

Roger, Alain. *Court traité du paysage*. Paris: Gallimard, 1997.

Rostaing, Charles. *Essai sur la toponymie en Provence* (Paris, 1950).

Schama, Simon. *Landscape and Memory*. New York: Alfred A. Knopf, 1995.

Sieburth, Richard. "Introduction: 'To Set Here the Roads of France.'" In *A Walking Tour in Southern France* by Ezra Pound. New York: New Directions, 1992.

Smithson, Robert. *The Collected Writings*. Berkeley: University of California Press, 1996.

Sobin, Gustaf. *Breaths' Burials*. New York: New Directions, 1995.

———. *The Earth as Air*. New York: New Directions, 1984.

———. *Luminous Debris: Reflecting on Vestige in Provence and Languedoc*. Berkeley: University of California Press, 1999.

———. *Towards the Blanched Alphabets*. Jersey City: Talisman House, 1998.

———. *Voyaging Portraits*. New York: New Directions, 1988.

Steinmetz, Jean-Luc. *Stéphane Mallarmé*. Paris: Fayard, 1998.

Thomas, Martin. *The Artificial Horizon: Imagining The Blue Mountains*. Melbourne: Melbourne University Press, 2003.

Thoreau, Henry David. *The Maine Woods*. 1864. Reprint, New York: Penguin, 1988.

———. *Walden*. 1854. Reprint: New York: Modern Library, 1950.

Veyne, Paul. *René Char en ses poèmes*. Paris: Gallimard, 1990.

Victoire, Honorin. *Petite Encyclopédie des Vents de France*. Paris: J. C. Lattès, 2001.

Weiss, Allen S. *Breathless: Sound Recording, Disembodiment, and the Transformation of Lyrical Nostalgia*. Middletown: Wesleyan University Press, 2002.

———. *Mirrors of Infinity: The French Formal Garden and 17th-Century Metaphysics*. New York: Princeton Architectural Press, 1995.

———. *Unnatural Horizons: Paradox and Contradiction in Landscape Architecture*. New York: Princeton Architectural Press, 1998.

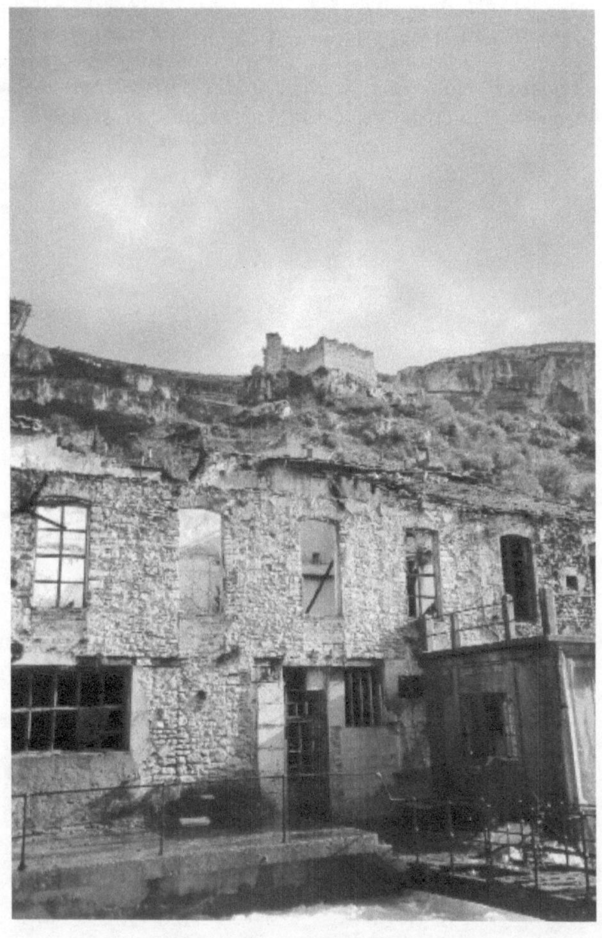

FIGURE 16. Fontaine-de-Vaucluse: Ruins of the paper mill (foreground) and of the chateau (background).

The grand source of pleasure in Fairy Tales is the natural desire to learn more of the Wonderland which is known to many as a word and nothing more . . .

Richard F. Burton, "Terminal Essay"
to his translation of *The Arabian Nights*

About the Author

ALLEN S. WEISS has written and edited over thirty books, including *The Aesthetics of Excess* (State University of New York Press); *Perverse Desire and the Ambiguous Icon* (State University of New York Press); *Mirrors of Infinity: The French Formal Garden and 17th-Century Metaphysics* (Princeton Architectural Press); *Phantasmic Radio* (Duke University Press); *Sade and the Narrative of Transgression* (Cambridge University Press); *Unnatural Horizons: Paradox and Contradiction in Landscape Architecture* (Princeton Architectural Press); *Experimental Sound and Radio* (Massachusetts Institute of Technology Press); *French Food* (Routledge); *Breathless: Sound Recording, Disembodiment, and the Transformation of Lyrical Nostalgia* (Wesleyan University Press); *Feast and Folly: Cuisine, Intoxication, and the Poetics of the Sublime* (State University of New York Press); *Poupées* (Gallimard); *Comment cuisiner un phénix* (Mercure de France). He directed both *Theater of the Ears,* a play for electronic marionette and taped voice based on the writings of Valère Novarina, and *Danse Macabre,* a marionette theater with the dolls of Michel Nedjar, and is completing a book of short stories, *The Aphoristic Theater*. He teaches in the Departments of Performance Studies and Cinema Studies at New York University.

Index

www.ingramcontent.com/pod-product-compliance
Lightning Source LLC
LaVergne TN
LVHW040156080826
844660LV00001B/2
9780791464892